W9-DFV-968

WITHDRAWN

Serena Williams

by Michael V. Uschan

LUCENT BOOKS

A part of Gale, Cengage Learning

GALE
CENGAGE Learning™

Detroit • New York • San Francisco • New Haven, Conn • Waterville, Maine • London

HUNTINGTON CITY TOWNSHIP
PUBLIC LIBRARY
255 WEST PARK DRIVE
HUNTINGTON, IN 46750

© 2011 Gale, Cengage Learning

ALL RIGHTS RESERVED. No part of this work covered by the copyright herein may be reproduced, transmitted, stored, or used in any form or by any means graphic, electronic, or mechanical, including but not limited to photocopying, recording, scanning, digitizing, taping, Web distribution, information networks, or information storage and retrieval systems, except as permitted under Section 107 or 108 of the 1976 United States Copyright Act, without the prior written permission of the publisher.

Every effort has been made to trace the owners of copyrighted material.

LIBRARY OF CONGRESS CATALOGING-IN-PUBLICATION DATA

Uschan, Michael V., 1948-
  Serena Williams / by Michael V. Uschan.
    p. cm. -- (People in the news)
  Includes bibliographical references and index.
  ISBN 978-1-4205-0488-0 (hardcover)
  1. Williams, Serena, 1981- 2. Women tennis players--United States--Biography. 3. African American women tennis players--Biography. I. Title.
  GV994.W55U63 2011
  796.342092--dc22
  [B]
                                                        2010033526

Lucent Books
27500 Drake Rd.
Farmington Hills, MI 48331

ISBN-13: 978-1-4205-0488-0
ISBN-10: 1-4205-0488-6

Printed in the United States of America
1 2 3 4 5 6 7 14 13 12 11 10

Printed by Bang Printing, Brainerd, MN, 1st Ptg., 01/2011

Contents

F ame and celebrity are alluring. People are drawn to those who walk in fame's spotlight, whether they are known for great accomplishments or for notorious deeds. The lives of the famous pique public interest and attract attention, perhaps because their experiences seem in some ways so different from, yet in other ways so similar to, our own.

Newspapers, magazines, and television regularly capitalize on this fascination with celebrity by running profiles of famous people. For example, television programs such as *Entertainment Tonight* devote all of their programming to stories about entertainment and entertainers. Magazines such as *People* fill their pages with stories of the private lives of famous people. Even newspapers, newsmagazines, and television news frequently delve into the lives of well-known personalities. Despite the number of articles and programs, few provide more than a superficial glimpse at their subjects.

Lucent's People in the News series offers young readers a deeper look into the lives of today's newsmakers, the influences that have shaped them, and the impact they have had in their fields of endeavor and on other people's lives. The subjects of the series hail from many disciplines and walks of life. They include authors, musicians, athletes, political leaders, entertainers, entrepreneurs, and others who have made a mark on modern life and who, in many cases, will continue to do so for years to come.

These biographies are more than factual chronicles. Each book emphasizes the contributions, accomplishments, or deeds that have brought fame or notoriety to the individual and shows how that person has influenced modern life. Authors portray their subjects in a realistic, unsentimental light. For example, Bill Gates—the cofounder and chief executive officer of the software giant Microsoft—has been instrumental in making personal computers the most vital tool of the modern age. Few dispute his business savvy, his perseverance, or his technical expertise, yet critics say he is ruthless in his dealings with competitors and driven more by his desire to maintain Microsoft's dominance in the computer industry than by an interest in furthering technology.

In these books, young readers will encounter inspiring stories about real people who achieved success despite enormous obstacles. Oprah Winfrey—the most powerful, most watched, and wealthiest woman on television today—spent the first six years of her life in the care of her grandparents while her unwed mother sought work and a better life elsewhere. Her adolescence was colored by promiscuity, pregnancy at age fourteen, rape, and sexual abuse.

Each author documents and supports his or her work with an array of primary and secondary source quotations taken from diaries, letters, speeches, and interviews. All quotes are footnoted to show readers exactly how and where biographers derive their information and provide guidance for further research. The quotations enliven the text by giving readers eyewitness views of the life and accomplishments of each person covered in the People in the News series.

In addition, each book in the series includes photographs, annotated bibliographies, timelines, and comprehensive indexes. For both the casual reader and the student researcher, the People in the News series offers insight into the lives of today's newsmakers—people who shape the way we live, work, and play in the modern age.

More than a Sports Superstar

What does Serena Williams have in common with President Barack Obama, former president Bill Clinton, singer Lady Gaga, computer inventor Steve Jobs, and former Alaska governor Sarah Palin? In 2010, *Time* magazine chose Williams and those other famous and powerful people as the one hundred most influential people in the world. The magazine's May 10 issue divided men and women who have heavily influenced recent history, popular culture, and the way people live into categories such as Leaders (Obama), Artists (Gaga), Thinkers (Jobs), and Heroes (Clinton). Williams joined Clinton as a hero for her work in promoting education in the United States and Africa, where she has helped build schools.

The magazine selected people in the same field as those honored to write articles that explained why each person chosen was worthy of being included on the list. Billie Jean King was the perfect choice to comment on the impact Williams has made on the world beyond her accomplishments in tennis. In addition to being a legendary tennis player, King was a pioneer in seeking equality for women in sports. This is what King wrote about Williams:

> Serena Williams is one of those rare champions who have transcended sports and impacted our society. In tennis, she is as focused [in 2010] as she has ever been at any point in her career [but she is also] committed to making a difference in the lives of others. Her work with children in

Kenya and here in the U.S. stresses the importance of education. Through her charitable efforts, people are seeing her in a larger context.[1]

It is not just her charitable work that has helped Williams impact the world far beyond the tennis courts on which she has won scores of tournaments since she began playing professionally at the age of fourteen. Because of the daring outfits she favors, Williams has brought a new, bolder style to the clothing tennis players and other female athletes wear. Williams has also etched her face and figure into the nation's cultural consciousness by appearing on television shows and music videos and being featured in advertisements in every medium.

Williams's greatest achievement, however, is one she shares with her older sister, Venus, who is also a tennis superstar. And that has been to shatter the color line in a sport that even late in the second half of the twentieth century was still played almost exclusively by whites.

Black Players, White Sport

When Richard Williams began teaching Venus and Serena how to play tennis as young children in Compton, California, his daughters were a rarity because so few African Americans played the sport. Because of that, the sisters were sometimes ridiculed by white players with whom they shared local public tennis courts. In her autobiography, Williams writes about an incident at Lynwood Park when she was six years old and Venus was seven. Williams writes that while their father, Richard, was instructing his daughters, some white children mocked them: "[A] group of kids started giving us a hard time. [Those] kids kept taunting us. They called us Blackie One and Blackie Two. It was so cruel, so arbitrary, but we kept playing. [I] don't think we heard those taunts as racist remarks. They were just taunts. Those kids were just being mean."[2]

Even though Williams chose not to consider the offensive remarks racist, she and her sister both understood that blacks have faced discrimination in the United States ever since the first African Ameri-

Serena Williams celebrates her victory in the 2010 Wimbledon singles championship.

cans arrived as indentured servants—a form of slavery—four centuries ago. In 1998 when Serena and Venus were being interviewed for a magazine article, they showed how much they knew about the historical roots of racism against blacks. In fact, they even surprised the reporter by explaining that Williams was not their real name but only the name of someone who had owned their ancestors:

"Williams is not even my real name," Venus [said].

"I beg your pardon?" [the reporter replied].

"I don't have a name," she says. "Williams is a slave owner's name."

"Our [real name and] other history has been taken from us," Serena adds.[3]

Their knowledge of black history also extended to the sport they would soon begin to dominate as two of the greatest women tennis players of all time. Only two blacks—Althea Gibson and Arthur Ashe—had ever won Grand Slam events, the four major tournaments played each year. In 1999 when Serena won the U.S. Open at the age of seventeen, she was the first black woman to claim a Grand Slam title since Gibson won the Open in 1958 and the first black since Ashe won Wimbledon in 1975. After her victory, Serena said she was happy Gibson had been there to see her win: "It's really amazing for me to have an opportunity to be compared to a player as great as Althea Gibson. One of her best friends told me she (Gibson) wanted to see another African-American win a Slam before her time is up. I'm so excited I had a chance to accomplish that while she's still alive."[4]

But breaking racial barriers in tennis—and even playing the sport itself—has been only one part of Serena's life. That's because she has never been content to be only a tennis player.

Not Just a Tennis Player

Most famous athletes are known only for what they accomplish in their chosen sports. A handful of stars, however, have such wide-ranging interests that they have become successful in other aspects of their lives. Williams's work in designing her own line of clothing, her appearances on television and other media, and her charity work have all helped her forge a global identity beyond tennis. In 2008, a reporter asked her, "Why is it not enough for you to be the best tennis player in the world?" This is how she answered: "Because there is so much more to me than just tennis. If you see my Hewlett Packard commercial you see what I mean. I'm more than just a tennis player. I'm a designer. I'm a thinker. I like to write. I like to do a lot of different things. While I'm doing all this stuff, I can still be a great tennis player."[5]

Chapter 1

Tennis: A Family Affair

A uthors often dedicate their books to people they love, respect, or who have played important roles in their lives, such as parents, spouses, or close friends. When *On the Line* was published in 2009, Serena Williams used the dedication in the autobiography to honor her father for all that he had done for her: "This book is dedicated to my daddy. Your vision and undying dedication made everything possible. I love you."[6] Serena singled out her dad because he was the person most responsible for molding her and her sister Venus into two of the best players in the history of women's tennis.

The dream that inspired Richard Dove Williams to help his daughters achieve such monumental success was born on June 11, 1978, while he was watching television. After he saw Virginia Ruzici receive a check for twenty-two thousand dollars for winning the French Open tennis championship, he exclaimed to his wife, Oracene, "That's what I earn in a year! Let's put our kids in tennis so they can become millionaires."[6] Williams was the stepfather of Lyndrea, Yetunde, and Isha, his wife's daughters from a previous marriage. Although they would not become the tennis stars he envisioned, two daughters yet to be born would.

Tennis stardom for his children was an unusual dream for an African American father to have because tennis was a sport played almost exclusively by whites, most of whom came from privileged backgrounds. In fact, Williams did not even know how to play tennis himself. Williams, however, would have the drive and talent to defy the odds stacked against him and make his dream a reality.

The Williams Family

Richard Williams was born in 1942 in Cedar Grove, a predominantly black section of Shreveport, Louisiana. Julia Mae Williams, his mother, raised him and his four sisters alone after his father abandoned the family. Julia supported her children by picking

(From left to right) Serena, Venus, their father Richard, and their mother Oracene attend Venus's professional tennis debut in Oakland, California, on October 31, 1994.

cotton and doing other jobs that required hard, physical labor. Although she was a strict disciplinarian, she lavished love on her children and told them they could achieve greatness by working hard for what they wanted. Life was difficult for the family because Julia did not make much money and because of the racism that existed in the southern states that limited the civil liberties of African Americans.

At age sixteen, Williams quit school. He moved around the country before eventually settling in Los Angeles, California. There African Americans enjoyed more opportunities for a better life because there was less racism than in the South. Although Williams was a dropout, he attended classes at Southwest College and the Los Angeles City School of Business so he could learn enough to one day run his own business. Richard met, fell in love with, and married Oracene Price, a nurse who had degrees in education and nursing from Eastern Michigan University.

Williams saw tennis as a way to help his stepdaughters and daughters have a better life than he had. Serena has written: "He had a tough time [as a child], but he was determined to keep his family from the same tough time."[8] Williams read books on tennis, watched instructional videos, and practiced daily with other men at a local tennis court. A good athlete who had played baseball and football while growing up in Shreveport, Williams easily developed into a solid player.

On June 17, 1980, Richard and Oracene had their first daughter together. Venus Ebony Starr was born in Lynwood, California, but not long after that the family moved to Oracene's hometown of Saginaw, Michigan. It was there, on September 26, 1981, that Serena Jameka Williams was born, one year, three months, and nine days after Venus. Less than two years later, in April 1983, the family returned to California and settled in Compton, a city with a population of 110,000 near Los Angeles. Richard started a private security firm and a telephone book delivery service, and the family bought a small home.

Oracene at first did not like Compton, a poor African American area with a high crime rate and the constant threat of violence. She explains why the city troubled her: "I never had the ghetto frame of mind. When I first moved there I hated it. Where I was raised [in Saginaw], we had trees and a house. It was nice. I was ashamed to say I lived in Compton. After a while I got used to it."[9]

It was in Compton, however, that Richard's tennis dream for his family would finally begin to become a reality.

Serena Learns to Play

When Venus was four years old, Richard began taking her to a nearby tennis court and teaching her to play the game he believed was his daughter's golden opportunity for fame and fortune. Three-year-old Serena accompanied her older sister to those lessons and soon began trying to play herself, even though she was not much bigger than the tennis racket Venus was trying to swing. In fact, those tennis outings involved the entire family and not just the two daughters who would grow up to make tennis history. In her autobiography, Serena writes: "It was a total family affair. There was me, my older sister Venus, and my mom and dad, together with our older sisters. [The] older girls had been playing for a time, while I had been trudging along [to watch them]."[10]

It was not long before little Serena herself had a chance to begin playing. After begging her dad constantly, he finally handed her a regulation racket and began tossing balls at her softly until she managed to hit a few of them. Serena at first missed most of the balls, but her dad kept encouraging her. Because Serena enjoyed the drill so much, that day marked the beginning of long training sessions for both of the girls. As they got older, Richard made the girls practice several hours almost every day of the week, sometimes requiring them to return five hundred or more balls that he hit at them. He also made the girls do other drills to learn the different strokes they needed to play tennis. Despite the grueling nature of the workouts, Serena explains that she and her sister enjoyed them because the girls knew that the drills would help make them better players: "Venus and I worked hard toward our goal from the very beginning. Dad and mom would load us, our racquets, a broom, and a bunch of milk crates filled with old tennis balls into our old red and white Volkswagen van, and we'd head off to practice tennis."[11]

First Tennis Memory

In her autobiography *On the Line*, Serena Williams writes about the first time she played tennis:

> My first tennis memory? [I] was three years old. It was a Saturday afternoon, maybe Sunday. My parents took us to the public courts at a park in Lynwood, California, not far from where we lived. There was me, my older sister Venus, and my mom and dad, together with our older sisters Lyndrea, Isha, and Yetunde. The older girls had been playing for a time, while I had been trudging along, but then one day my dad announced I was ready to take my swings, too. He put a standard, regulation-size racket in my hand and positioned me a couple feet from the net. Then he climbed to the other side and started soft-tossing until I managed to hit a couple over. "Just look at the ball, Serena," he kept saying, in that patient tone I'd come to hear in my dreams. "Just swing." Daddy believed tennis was our ticket up and out of Compton, but he also knew we had to take to it. He knew it wasn't enough simply to teach us the game and train us to be champions. We had to have some God-given talent and athletic ability. We had to develop a passion for the game and an iron will to succeed.

Serena Williams with Daniel Paisner, *On the Line*. Boston: Grand Central, 2009, p. 9.

The Williams family practiced on courts at a nearby public park. Unlike the pristine courts on which most youngsters their age played, the asphalt surfaces in Compton were in poor shape and had grass growing through small cracks. The courts were sometimes littered with broken glass and drug paraphernalia that the girls had to sweep away before they could play. Local street gangs who used the courts as a gathering place resented their presence, and a gang member once fired shots at them, forcing them to dive for safety. That scary incident happened when Venus was nine and Serena was just eight years old. In 1991, Richard

Getting Shot At

The public court in Compton, California, on which Richard Williams taught his daughters Serena and Venus to play tennis was used by local gang members who sometimes shot at each other. A magazine article discusses how even the threat of such violence could not stop the Williams family from pursuing its tennis dream:

> Gradually, Richard befriended the local gang members, and the three Williamses became fixtures on the Compton courts. One day [when Venus was nine and Serena eight], a gang lieutenant stood up through the sunroof of his car and sprayed the courts with bullets. Venus and Serena dived for cover. Richard told the girls not to say anything to Oracene. But when they got home, they announced what had happened. "Mama, we got shot at," they chirped. "Did my girls get shot at?" Oracene demanded [of her husband]. "You know how kids are," Richard said. "They're not joking," Oracene said. "I better not catch my kids down there again." The next evening Richard took Oracene out for dinner. As they walked through the neighborhood near East Compton Park, they watched police chase down an overweight local boy. Oracene wanted to intervene. "That's not right," she said. But Richard pointedly countered, "Why should we do anything? After all, we ain't coming back to this park." Oracene got the message: They were a part of the neighborhood, for better or worse. The next day, she took the girls to the park herself.

Sally Jenkins, "Double Trouble," *Women's Sports & Fitness*, November/December 1998, p. 102.

The Compton, California, tennis court where Serena and Venus played and where they were shot at by local gang members.

told a reporter about the dangers he and his daughters had faced to learn tennis: "We play in hell. We've been shot at on the tennis court. But now gang members know us and protect us when the shooting starts."[12] Richard said gang members began doing that after he explained to them that he was trying to do something positive for his daughters.

Oracene and her older daughters often tagged along to watch Venus and Serena and retrieve balls during the practice sessions so they could hit them. It was only natural that they did that—the Williams family did almost everything together.

Serena "the Princess"

The small Williams home was so crowded that all five sisters had to sleep in one room. The mathematics of their sleeping arrangements—they had two bunk beds, which meant there were four beds for five sisters—made them even more close-knit. The two oldest sisters—Isha and Yetunde—got the two top bunk beds while Lyn and Venus claimed the lower ones. As the youngest sibling, Serena had to sleep with a different sister every night. She did not mind sharing a bed because she loved her sisters. In fact, Serena has written that her sisters all played important but different roles in her childhood: "Tunde was the forgiver; she had a heart of gold. Isha was the caretaker; she looked after each of us. Lyn was our play pal [and] Venus was my protector [who was] on constant lookout for any situation that might cause me trouble or distress. And me, I was the princess; I was everyone's pet."[13]

Even though Richard was grooming Serena and Venus as tennis stars, he and Oracene still made them study hard in school. Their parents demanded they get nothing but A's and if they failed to do that they could not practice tennis, which they loved. The sisters also had to do household chores such as clearing dinner dishes and cleaning the house. Attending church was another requirement. Oracene was a Jehovah's Witness, and all her daughters adopted her faith. That Christian sect has strict rules about behavior, including not celebrating birthdays and religious holidays, and it endorses a literal interpretation of the Bible. Serena once explained her faith to a reporter:

We believe that God inspired men on earth at the time to write the Bible. And so the Bible is his word. Mostly, we believe in the Bible. Our basic belief comes from the Bible. So we don't believe in idolatry, fornication, things like that. We believe that God's original purpose with mankind was to have a paradise [on earth].[14]

Serena's religious beliefs and strict upbringing by her parents made her behave while she was growing up. "I've always tried to be respectful of my parents," Serena said as an adult. "We were all pretty good kids. I never sneaked out windows [and] I've never talked back to my mom."[15] But Serena was not always a good little girl. When Serena was young, her father was talking to his daughters about how important it was to admit when they had done something wrong. Serena took that message to heart and told him that the previous week she had thrown his dentures away, which he thought he had lost. Her dad gave her a spanking for misbehaving.

Richard, however, was rarely mad at Serena about her tennis because she and Venus worked so hard to become good players. And within a few years, they shocked the tennis world with how talented they were.

The Unknown Stars

Because their father trained Venus and Serena on the nearly deserted Compton courts, few people realized how good they were becoming. That changed when he started having them compete in tournaments for young players. Venus began playing at age nine. To the surprise of people knowledgeable about California tennis, a tall, skinny, young black girl—Venus was five-feet, four-inches (1.63m) tall and weighed 80 pounds (36kg)—whom they had never heard of nor seen play began beating everyone. From the age of nine to eleven, Venus was undefeated in sixty-three matches, often against players older than herself.

Serena was proud of her big sister but yearned to compete herself, and she kept begging her father to let her play in a tournament. She became so frustrated that she secretly entered a tournament Venus was going to play in for girls ten and younger. When Serena's

At age nine, Serena slams a serve at the Nancy Reagan Tennis Tournament.

Venus Williams came off her Compton tennis court (pictured)
to win the Southern California Championships for girls twelve
and under when she was ten.

name was called to compete on the day of the tournament, her dad was shocked because he had not known she had entered it. But Richard let her play and she won the match. "Meeka!" he said using his nickname for her. "Look at you! You won! You played great!"[16] To her dad's amazement, Serena kept beating older players and made it to the final match. Unfortunately, her opponent was her sister Venus, who easily defeated her 6–2, 6–2 in the first of many confrontations to come between the two powerful players. Even though Serena lost to Venus, she was happy just to have competed. She was also excited because of the attention she got from spectators who flocked to see the newcomer.

Although Serena was not as invincible as Venus, she lost only three of fifty matches in the next few years. When a reporter asked Serena what she enjoyed most about playing, she fired back, "Winning. I like going out and beating up on people. I get joy out of that. I really do."[17]

Brash statements like that set Serena and Venus apart from other players who usually adopted a more humble attitude. Their father was far bolder in talking about his talented daughters and predicted they would become the game's best players. Most people believed his predictions seemed more fantasy than reality because Venus and Serena were African Americans in a sport in which only a handful of blacks, like Althea Gibson and Arthur Ashe, had ever become stars. This is how Serena explained the strange attitude people had toward her and Venus when they first burst upon the public scene and began to amaze people with their superior talent:

> Our father was going around telling people we would be the best tennis players in the world. He started calling Venus a "ghetto Cinderella." I'm sure a lot of people thought that he was crazy—and that we were, too. I mean, people were used to seeing tennis champions who were white. Who was ever going to believe that two black girls from Compton could become the best in the world?[18]

Richard's brazen statements began to come true in 1990 when ten-year-old Venus won the Southern California championships for girls twelve and younger. Because California has so many talented players, the victory brought her national fame. Venus, just a fifth-grade student, was featured on the front page of the prestigious *New York Times* newspaper in a story that also mentioned her talented younger sister.

Dad Was "a Genius"

Richard's statements about how successful his daughters would be upset some people because bragging was unusual in tennis. And when newspaper and magazine stories explained how he had single-handedly molded his daughters into tennis players,

Tennis Scoring

Tennis scoring is complicated and has unusual terms. Players compete until one player wins a set or has won two out of three or three out of five sets. A set consists of at least six games. The winner's score in a set could range from 6–0, in which the player wins every game, to 6–4 in which the defeated opponent manages to capture four games. A player has to win a set by at least two games, so if players are tied at 5–5 they continue to play until someone wins by a score such as 7–5 or 8–6. In some competitions, only a single tie-breaker game is required to win a set, as in sudden death in football. Scoring in a single game can also seem complicated to newcomers. A player needs four points to win a single game and the terms for the points are 15, 30, 40, and game. If one player wins the first point, the score is called 15–love, with love meaning zero. The opposing player's score remains love until the player wins a point. As in a set, a player must win a game by two points. If players are tied at 40, it is called deuce, and they have to play until someone wins by the required margin. The player who wins the first point after deuce is said to "have the advantage" because they can win the game by winning the next point. If the opponent wins the next point, the score is again deuce.

some people criticized him for forcing Venus and Serena to play tennis. But Serena never felt her father had pushed them into tennis against their will, and as an adult she defended him against such criticism. She said, "My dad is the nicest guy you'll ever meet, and the easiest going. My dad really is a genius to get me and my sister in tennis."[19] The truth was that Richard did not have to force his daughters to play tennis, because they loved the game.

Chapter 2

Preparing for the Pros

One week before her eleventh birthday, the June 10, 1991, edition of *Sports Illustrated* magazine featured a story on Venus Williams that claimed she might be the best young player in the history of tennis. The article briefly mentioned her talented younger sister, Serena, and detailed how Richard Williams had single-handedly transformed his daughters into future tennis stars. Richard normally relished any praise he received for teaching them and enjoyed taking the lion's share of the media spotlight for their success. But he uncharacteristically admitted to the magazine that he had done as much as he could to help Venus become the best player she could be. "Her skills have already passed me," he said. "I need someone to give her better practice and take her to the next level."[20]

His statement also applied to Serena, who trailed her older sister in developing as a player even though she was nearly invincible against opponents she had faced in junior tournaments. Richard said he was considering two options—to have a California professional teach his daughters or go to Florida and enroll them in one of several tennis academies that trained most of the nation's best young players. A few months later, in September, Richard made his decision—he uprooted his family and moved to Florida so his daughters could take lessons at the Rick Macci International Tennis Academy in Del Ray Beach. Macci had wooed the Williams family by coming to Compton to watch Venus play and to explain how he could help her. But when he told Richard "it looks like you have

Ten-year-old Venus Williams talks with her coach Rick Macci on the practice court before her professional debut at the Bank of the West Classic on October 31, 1994.

the next Michael Jordan on your hands," the proud father replied, "No, Mr. Macci, we've got the next *two* Michael Jordans,"[21] meaning both Venus *and* Serena.

The Florida move began a period of several years in which Venus and Serena disappeared almost entirely from the public spotlight. They would not emerge from the seclusion imposed on them by their father until they were ready to play professional tennis.

Protecting His Daughters

When Richard moved his family to Florida, he made a decision that amazed people in the tennis establishment—he decided his daughters would no longer compete in junior tournaments. He did not like the atmosphere at the tournaments because so many parents went crazy cheering their children and even rooting against players their kids faced. Richard also admitted that he did not like junior tournaments because of racism his daughters sometimes encountered. He told a reporter that "when a white girl lost to my daughter, the parent would say, 'You let me down. How could you let that little n----- beat you?' I didn't want my kids growing up around that."[22]

Even though many tennis experts believed the sisters needed to keep competing against players their own age, Richard felt they had already shown they knew how to handle the pressure of competition by virtue of their California tournament records—Venus was 63–0 and Serena 43–7 in individual matches. Serena said years later that her dad made the right decision for his daughters: "He didn't like the way parents [and] coaches were all over their junior players [and] wanted us to have a normal life. [And] he

Venus and Serena ran up 63–0 and 43–7 records respectively, on the California tennis scene. Here they pose with President Ronald Reagan and his wife Nancy on October 6, 1990.

thought we could get better competition, just hitting with these pros and coaches and working on our fundamentals. I've always thought this was a genius move."[23]

The normal life Richard wanted for Venus and Serena included going to school because he and Oracene demanded that they work hard in their classes even though they would be training hard. By not competing in tournaments, which required extensive travel, they would have more time to study, pursue other interests, and have time with their family.

Preparing for the Pros

The Macci school had a reputation for developing young players like Jennifer Capriati into teenage tennis stars. When she turned pro on March 5, 1990, three weeks before her fourteenth birthday, many people doubted she was old enough or good enough to compete against adults. But in Capriati's first tournament, she defeated four quality opponents to become the youngest player in history to reach the title match in a professional tournament. Even though she lost to Gabriela Sabatini 6–4, 7–5 in the championship final, her remarkable accomplishment shocked the tennis world and spurred other teenagers to think about turning professional.

Macci shared responsibility for the sisters' overall development with their father, who continued to help teach his daughters on a daily basis. Because Venus was so far ahead of Serena, Macci concentrated on improving Venus's skills. The sisters also worked with Dave Rineberg, a hitting coach who taught them how to perform various shots. He also practiced against the girls to get them accustomed to playing a superior opponent, which Rineberg was when he was younger. Rineberg remembers that he was amazed at how athletic Serena and Venus were the first time he saw them play:

> [The] power [of their shots] I had heard about was nothing compared to the athletic movements of these girls. In one rally, Venus crossed the entire court with two panther-like bounds and ripped a two-handed backswing down the line for a winner. In another rally, Serena chased down a drop

shot and then a lob, before hitting a swinging volley to win the point. The talent was raw, but it was pure.[24]

The tennis academy also stressed overall fitness and strength development to make players better. Both sisters were already very strong and athletic. Venus had been a promising runner, and when she was eight ran a mile in five minutes, eight seconds, a phenomenal time for someone so young. Serena enjoyed gymnastics. The fitness regime included running and weight lifting, which Serena hated but did anyway to become a better player. Good nutrition is part of having a strong body, and Venus said her parents had already taught her and her sister that they had to eat the right foods to become great athletes: "When Serena and I were growing up, our mom and dad didn't let us eat a lot of junk food—cookies, cakes, pre-sweetened cereals, candy, potato chips, pork rinds, and ice cream. In fact, they wouldn't even bring it into the house. [We] were really lucky that our parents made us eat healthy."[25]

During this period Venus was the unrivaled family star. Even though Venus received more direct training from coaches in this period, Serena was never jealous of the attention her older sister got. One reason is that Richard was working with her more on a daily basis, and she enjoyed the extra time she was able to spend learning tennis from her father. Said Serena: "For me, that was one of the great benefits of being on the second string, in terms of everyone's expectations: I finally had my dad to myself."[26]

A Busy Life

Venus and Serena practiced tennis five or six hours daily, six days a week. They were able to start about 1 P.M. because the family had an arrangement with Carver Middle School to allow their daughters to leave early. To make up for the shorter school day, the girls were given extra homework, and their parents made sure they did it every night. In 1993 Richard and Oracene took control of their education and began homeschooling Venus and Serena. Macci said that even though Richard always pushed his daughters hard in practice, he sometimes put their need to study

First Impressions

Starting in December 1992, Dave Rineberg was the hitting coach of Venus and Serena Williams, a position he held for seven years. He taught them how to hit shots and played against them to teach them on-court strategy. In a book about his experience with the Williams sisters, Rineberg describes the first time he met them. He says he was not only impressed by the intensity with which they played but how polite they were when their father Richard introduced them to him. Rineberg writes that Venus introduced herself first and then her younger sister, who seemed more shy:

> "Hi, I am Venus. It is nice to meet you." I noticed the politeness. What a welcome change. I was teaching about eight hours of junior tennis a week and only a few of my students had such good manners. ... "Hi, I am Serena." She was polite also, but her physique was smaller [than her sister's] and more solid. She seemed to shy away quickly. Maybe she was just stepping back into Venus's shadow where she felt more comfortable. Both girls kissed their father and then started slapping the ball back and forth, as if they were in a third set of the U.S. Open finals.

Dave Rineberg, Venus & Serena: *My Seven Years as Hitting Coach for the Williams Sisters.* Hollywood, CA: Frederick Fell, 2001.

ahead of learning how to play: "[He's] always been an incredible father to those two girls. [I] can remember fifty times when he called off practice because Venus's grades were down. They'd be in my office studying French, and I'd be saying, "Hey, we've got to work."[27]

Because Venus and Serena were so busy studying and playing tennis, their parents limited their free time. They could only watch two hours of television a week and were not allowed to go to parties. And when Serena was nine and Venus eleven, they went to bed at 9 P.M. to make sure they got enough rest for their rigorous tennis and school schedules. Their lives were not all

Though the girls practiced six hours a day, six days a week, Richard and Oracene made sure the girls' studies did not suffer. Richard always tried to make practice enjoyable for his daughters.

hard work. Rineberg remembers that Richard always tried to make practice enjoyable for his daughters so they would not get bored. Rineberg also said Richard sometimes canceled practice and took his daughters to nearby Disney World so they could relax. As Macci relates: "He was good at keeping it fun for them. He used to say that he believed it was family first, then education, then religion, and then maybe tennis. The bottom line was, Richard was going to be a parent first and his coaching and managing would all be second."[28]

Although Richard did not want his daughters competing on the junior circuit, he occasionally allowed them to play publicly in special events. One was the Family Circle Magazine Cup at Hilton Head, South Carolina, a professional event famed for having showcased young stars like Gabriela Sabatini, Steffi Graf, and Chris Evert. On April 5, 1992, ten-year-old Serena and eleven-year-old Venus played against each other while teaming with pros Billie Jean King and Rosie Casals in an exhibition doubles match.

Serena and King, one of the most influential female players in tennis history, won the match. Afterward, King expressed her amazement at how good the sisters were at such a young age. "I don't think I even knew what tennis was at that age, but the important thing is that they go slowly and do the right thing. That's what makes champions."[29]

Richard wanted his daughters to move slowly in preparing for their professional careers. The problem was that the huge potential Venus and Serena had to be future stars made it hard for them to remain amateurs.

Fame and Money

The news media kept writing stories about Venus and Serena even though they were not competing in junior tournaments. Media interest was fueled not only by the talent the sisters had already displayed at such a young age but by the fact that they were African Americans in a mostly white sport. Nick Bollettieri, whose Florida tennis academy had attracted many top young players, explained that her race made Venus a valuable commodity: "The sporting goods companies are looking for the rarity, and being a minority athlete, Venus could have it made."[30]

The fame the news coverage brought them and their vast potential for future success also captured the attention of professional sports agents, who believed the sisters could earn huge amounts of money by endorsing products like tennis equipment. The agents wanted to represent them because they receive a percentage of any business deals they arrange for their clients. And the girls' earning potential was huge. Within a year after Capriati turned pro in 1990, she had signed contracts worth an estimated $10 million, and agents believed Venus and Serena could make even more money.

Most of the attention was focused on Venus, who developed more quickly than her younger sister. When Venus was only ten years old and in the fifth grade, top sports agents were already trying to persuade her dad to sign a contract. Richard said agents were promising him homes, cars, and millions of dollars to sign Venus. There were so many offers that even before Richard moved the family to Florida he had asked lawyers Keven Davis and Sally

Teen Sensations

In the 1980s and early 1990s, tennis changed dramatically when a series of young players turned professional and began winning tournaments. No sport had ever seen so many young men and women players have so much success playing for money against players far older and more experienced than they were. And the success young stars like Michael Chang, Pete Sampras, Arantxa Sánchez Vicario, and Monica Seles had led more and more young players to consider turning pro when they were teenagers still in high school. Not everyone, however, believed it was good for such young players to do that. Patricio Apey worked for ProServ, a sports agency that represents athletes. In a 1991 newspaper story on young players turning pro, Apey said that in 1990 he went to France to battle International Management Group, another sports agency, for twelve-and-a-half-year-old Magnus Norman of Sweden, who was ready to turn professional. Apey admitted it bothered him that such a young player wanted to start playing for money against adults, and he joked that "the next thing you know we'll [sports agents] be running into each other in the maternity ward at the hospital outside the incubators."

Robin Finn, "In Tennis, Child Prodigies Whet the Agents' Appetites," *New York Times*, April 8, 1991, p. C6.

Sullivan to help him in assessing them. Although Richard admitted it would be nice to have so much money, he said he would not sign deals because he worried they could hurt Venus:

> [If] we sign her to a professional contract when she's ten, what will she do between now and when she's thirteen, when she can actually play the professional circuit? I don't want her to peak at twelve and fall to pieces at fifteen. There's still a lot of ifs here [and] nobody in this house is going to push our daughter into anything.[31]

Venus herself, however, was already planning to play professionally. In November 1993 when she was thirteen, a newspaper story described her as a bright eighth-grader who was studying French and Spanish because they were languages she could use when she played professional tournaments in Europe. Venus also explained her own timetable for the future: "I want to turn pro when I'm fifteen. I don't want to go too early or too late."[32]

But a rules change by the Women's Tennis Association (WTA), the governing body for professional women's tennis, would speed up her debut as a professional player.

Venus Turns Pro

In 1994 the Women's Tennis Association raised the age women could turn professional. The WTA ruled that starting in 1995 the minimum age for a professional would be fifteen, one year older than previously, and that minimum age would keep rising annually until it hit eighteen. The rule also limited the number of tournaments younger players could play each year until they turned eighteen. The WTA raised the age because some young players had encountered problems dealing with the pro lifestyle. Among them was Capriati, who was arrested in 1993 for shoplifting a thirty-five-dollar ring even though she had made millions of dollars. Then she was arrested again in 1994 for marijuana possession.

The WTA, however, had a clause that allowed players who were close to becoming fourteen to turn professional earlier. Because Venus would turn fourteen on June 17, 1994, she decided she would turn pro to beat the new age restrictions. Her father was against Venus becoming a pro so early but said he would let her do what she wanted. "It's my feeling that a 14-year-old shouldn't play, but this is her decision, so she's going to turn professional on her home ground in California."[33] The family chose the Bank of the West Classic in Oakland, California, for her professional debut.

Venus had not played a competitive match for several years, but on October 31 she defeated Shaun Stafford, the fifty-ninth-ranked player in the world, 6–3, 6–4. "For her to be that good at 14 is awesome," Stafford said in praise of Venus. "When I was 14, I was immature, but this girl's mature. It's good to see she is in fact ready for the pros."[34] In the second round, Venus faced Arantxa Sánchez Vicario, the world's second-ranked player. Although

Venus Turns Pro

In her autobiography, Serena Williams describes how thrilled she was when Venus played her first professional match on October 31, 1994:

> I remember it as such an exciting moment, such an exciting time. We didn't have enough money for all of us to travel from Florida, but I went as Venus's hitting partner. Lyn came, too. What a thrill! To be down on those courts with all those great players! Oh my goodness, I was so pumped! Daddy told me to hit as hard as I could when I was working with Venus, and I imagined that I was playing in the tournament and that Venus was the top seed and that all these people were watching us and cheering for us. [I] can't even tell you how happy I was for V [when she won her first match]. I was over the moon and back again. It was crazy! The win earned Venus a whopping $5,350 in prize money —which was just about a fortune to her at the time. Daddy's idea was to let us keep all the money we earned, and to learn to be responsible for it right away, so Venus started to look really, really rich in my eyes, and I was only too happy to let her spoil me.

Serena Williams with Daniel Paisner, *On the Line*. Boston: Grand Central, 2009, p. 111–12.

Venus, fourteen, in action during her professional debut at the Bank of the West Classic in Oakland, California, on October 31, 1994

By the time of Venus's pro debut, Serena was developing into a great tennis player in her own right. Practicing against each other made them both better.

Venus won the first set, the Spaniard battled back to win the next two sets and the match 6–3, 6–0.

Serena Ready, Too

Serena was excited for her sister and thrilled she had traveled to California as her sister's hitting partner to help Venus prepare for the competition. When reporters besieged Richard with questions about Venus, he was happy to answer them all. But he also asked them "Have you seen my other daughter Serena play? She's better than Venus."[35] It would not be long before Serena would make her own professional debut to show the world what she could do.

HUNTINGTON CITY TOWNSHIP
PUBLIC LIBRARY
255 WEST PARK DRIVE
HUNTINGTON, IN 46750

Chapter 3

Escaping from Her Sister's Shadow

L ife did not change much for Serena Williams after Venus made her professional debut. The sisters continued practicing tennis together in Florida because Venus did not play professionally again until August 1995 in Los Angeles, where she lost a first round match. This time it was hard for Serena to watch her sister because she envied Venus's status as a pro. In her 2009 autobiography Serena notes: "I wanted to be out there playing, making noise of my own. I wanted what Venus had and I didn't want to wait for it to be my turn. I wanted it right away."[36] As it turned out, Serena did not have to wait long to get her wish.

When Serena celebrated her fourteenth birthday on September 26, she faced a critical decision about her future. If she did not play a professional tournament by the end of 1995, the Women's Tennis Association (WTA) age rule for players would force Serena to remain an amateur until she was sixteen and would then restrict the number of tournaments she could play until she was eighteen. So Serena convinced her parents to let her turn pro even though they were not sure she was ready for that level of competition.

On October 31, Serena played Anne Miller at the Bell Challenge in Quebec City, Canada. Unlike Venus who had won in her professional debut, Serena was humbled 6–1, 6–1 in less than an hour by a player four years older than she was. Serena recalls, "I felt bad out there because I lost. I played kind of like an amateur."

But the teenager was not cowed by her poor showing and defiantly told reporters: "I've practiced tennis since I was four, and I practiced to play on the professional tour level, not the amateur. I feel like I'm more ready than ever to get out here and compete with the professionals. Once I make a decision, I never go back on it."[37]

Despite Serena's shaky start, hitting coach Dave Rineberg claimed years later that "Serena's path to the pros was a paved superhighway compared to [that of her sister because Venus] had blazed a trail for success."[38] Serena's rise to stardom, however, would be slower than that of Venus's and would keep her in the secondary role of the younger, less-talented sister longer than she would have liked.

Serena practices as her father looks on. The decision to go pro early was prompted by new World Tennis Association rules for younger players.

Taking It Slowly

Richard and Oracene Williams had spent more than a decade grooming their daughters for professional tennis. But after her daughters made it to the pros, Oracene admitted she was not sure if that had been the right choice for them. Oracene claimed, "I wanted them to wait until they were sixteen [because] I worry about

Serena grimaces in pain from a sprained ankle in her 1997 Ameritech Cup semifinal loss to Lindsay Davenport. Though she lost, it was clear that Serena was emerging from her sister's shadow.

them starting out quick and fizzling out early."[39] To make sure their daughters did not lose interest in tennis or develop personal problems like some teens who had turned pro early, Oracene and Richard limited the girls playing schedules for the next few years.

In 1996 Venus played without much success in five tournaments, and Serena did not play professionally at all as she concentrated on improving enough to be competitive as a professional. But in 1997, the sisters began to show the talent that had led Richard to boast that each of his daughters could one day become the world's best player. In October at the Ameritech Cup in Chicago, Serena defeated Monica Seles and Mary Pierce. She made history as the lowest-ranked player—304th in the world—to record her first career wins over two players in the top ten in the world rankings. Seles was the world's number 4 player and Pierce number 7. Although Serena lost to Lindsay Davenport in the semifinals, it was a fantastic performance for a sixteen-year-old. It was also one that allowed her to emerge from her sister's shadow as a good player in her own right. "I'm not just her little sister anymore,"[40] she told reporters.

Venus's own breakthrough season was highlighted by her sensational run to the title match of the U.S. Open, one of four annual Grand Slam events that are the most important in tennis. But Martina Hingis, a sixteen-year-old and a year younger than Venus, defeated her 6–0, 6–4 for the title. That loss, however, was not Venus's most publicized match. Her semifinal win over Romanian player Irina Spirlea generated a media firestorm of controversy, including charges of racism by Richard Williams. The incident also made public the problems the two sisters had experienced in getting along with other players.

A Williams Sisters Backlash

The 1997 U.S. Open in Flushing Meadows, New York, was supposed to celebrate the racial diversity the once all-white sport had finally achieved in the twentieth century. The competition was played in a new stadium named after Arthur Ashe and began on the seventieth birthday of Althea Gibson, the two most successful African American players in tennis history. In the semifinal match, Spirlea intentionally collided with Venus while they were changing sides of the court between games; Venus was winning at the time Spirlea bumped her. Richard Williams claimed Spirlea's action was racially motivated—he used racial terms himself by calling her "a big, ugly, tall, white turkey"—but Spirlea said afterward that she did it because she believed Venus was acting haughty, partly because of all the media attention she got because she was a rising African American star in a sport dominated by whites.

The incident publicized player animosity toward the sisters that had been previously known only by tennis insiders. Although Richard did not single out Spirlea, he claimed after the incident that he had heard some professional players use the racist N-word to refer to his daughters. After Venus lost to Hingis in the title match, the news media questioned her about her dad's claim of racism. Venus tried to evade the question. She answered that since the tournament was supposed to have been about racial harmony, "I think this is definitely ruining the mood, these questions about racism."[41] When reporters continued querying her, she fled the interview session.

Although some players may have disliked blacks, most observers claimed racism was not the main reason why Venus and Serena were having trouble being accepted by other players. One problem they faced in making friends was the jealousy other players had over their swift rise to fame and fortune. In 1995 when Anne Miller defeated Serena in her pro debut, Miller had sarcastically commented, "I guess I played a celebrity."[42] The remark showed how much players envied the mass media attention Venus and Serena had received as African Americans succeeding in a white sport. The fame the sisters received from the media coverage also helped them win huge endorsement contracts that most other players could only dream about, and that made them even more envious of the sisters. In May 1995 Reebok signed Venus to a contract worth $12 million to endorse its sports line, and in January 1998 Serena landed a similar deal with Puma.

Another problem the sisters had in being accepted was that they were so close they did not need anyone else for companionship. Their father once famously claimed that he did not think they needed anyone else, and Serena had remarked how grateful

Racism

In a 1998 magazine article, sportswriter Sally Jenkins wrote about how racism affected Serena and Venus Williams:

> The truth is that there is racism in tennis, and it has been directed at the Williamses, although it has rarely been explicit. Rather, it has been conveyed by innuendo and insinuation, and in a subtle disproportion in the way people respond to them, alternating between vitriol and over-congratulation. "People talk about how smart and articulate Venus is," says their attorney Keven Davis, "as if it's surprising. Why? Because judgments are already made. People don't expect her to be able to talk [because she is black]." The racism lies in the fact that everyone thought Richard was wrong—that Venus and Serena would fail. It lies in the way commentators call Venus the "Tiger Woods [a black golfer] of tennis," when a more appropriate comparison would be to Chris Evert, the last homegrown American woman to win a Grand Slam title (in 1986). It lies in the fact that historically there have been so few prominent black tennis players—Althea Gibson, Arthur Ashe, Zina Garrison, MaliVai Washington, Lori McNeil and Chanda Rubin—that Venus and Serena are inevitably identified not by talent or nationality but by race. "Good luck," says Garrison, a former Wimbledon finalist who retired in 1996. "I was ranked No. 4 in the world, and I was still known as the black American tennis player."

Sally Jenkins, "Double Trouble," *Women's Sports & Fitness*, November/December 1998, p. 102.

she was to have a sister like Venus: "It's fun. You've always got someone to hang out with. Sometimes people join us. They never last long. It's always been just Venus and I."[43] This attitude angered some players. Lindsay Davenport once criticized Venus for not returning smiles or greetings in the locker room. Davenport also claimed that it was the way Venus acted that caused friction

Venus and Serena at the 1997 U.S. Open. Despite being a tournament that promoted racial harmony, their father Richard says the girls faced racism from other players.

between her and other players. "I don't feel it's a problem of race. I feel like Venus has separated herself from us for whatever reason,"[44] Davenport said.

But in 1998, sportswriter Sally Jenkins wrote that it was not unusual for players as talented as Venus and Serena to remain aloof from their competitors: "The truth in all of this is that top players are rarely sociable in the locker room. The truth is that Venus and Serena can be defensive and hostile just like most great players." Former African American tour player Zina Garrison also told Jenkins, "How much acceptance do you really need when you're trying to reach the top?"[45]

Their unfriendly attitude toward competitors did not extend to each other. When they met as professionals for the first time in January 1998, Venus defeated Serena in the Australian Open. Afterward, Venus was overheard telling her sister, "I'm sorry I had to take you out, Serena."[46] But they continued battling other players and occasionally each other to pursue their dreams of becoming

Star Power

The emergence of Serena Williams as a great player in 1999 helped the two sisters reach new heights of global fame. The November 1999 issue of *Tennis* magazine noted the star power that Venus and Serena shared:

> It's no stretch to say that tennis has seldom, if ever, seen media stars like the Williams sisters. [Even] before they rose to career-high rankings of No. 3 (Venus) and No. 4 (Serena), they'd already become the sport's most marketable faces. Together, the Williamses have made tennis an in-your-face game, and their brash comments—"I think everyone I play is intimidated by me," says Serena—have become the norm. Though much is made, and rightly so, of their being role models for other African-Americans, their appeal crosses age, gender, and racial lines. At the 1999 Lipton Championships, the Williams' trademark beaded hairstyles inspired tournament organizers to set up a booth where you could be made to look just like them—for $5 a braid. Even away from the courts, a sighting of Venus or Serena is enough to stop a taxi driver, an elderly gift-shop clerk, a little girl in tennis gear, and a middle-aged couple, one of whom introduces herself as a psychic. "Other people say we're [arrogant], but we're really not," Serena says before rushing off for her one-on-one with Jay Leno. "We say it and we mean it. We know how to get what we want."

Johnette Howard, "Bragging Rights," *Tennis*, November 1999, p. 36.

At the 1999 Lipton Championships, the Williams sisters' beaded hairstyle was the fashion rage. It signified their star appeal across age, gender, and racial lines.

the highest-ranked player in the world. In the process, they began making tennis history.

Sisters Like No Other

On March 1, 1999, Serena defeated Amelie Mauresmo 6–2, 3–6, 7–6 to win her first tournament, the Gaz de France in Paris. Just a few hours later and several thousand miles away, Venus won the IGA Superthrift Classic in Oklahoma City, Oklahoma. The twin wins made them the first sisters to win tournaments on the same day. The victory was Venus's fourth tournament title. But Serena had the satisfaction of capturing her first singles title at the age of seventeen years and five months, which made her three months younger than Venus had been when she clinched her first victory.

It was unusual for the sisters to make history while far apart because they were almost always together. During their forced separation, they chatted back and forth online and called each other. Serena tried to contact Venus after her victory but told reporters Venus couldn't be reached: "I wasn't able to talk to her yet, but I did talk to my dad, who told me some things. I'll see Venus soon."[47] The sisters apparently never tired of each other either on or off the court.

When Serena and Venus were not on the road playing tournaments, they practiced together three to four hours a day, five days a week with their dad and other coaches. They lived together in a home they built in 1999 not far from where their parents lived. For fun, the sisters liked to surf, ride jet skis, and in-line skate. After being homeschooled for several years, they both graduated from Driftwood Academy—Venus in 1998 and Serena in 1999. Driftwood is a thirty-student private high school, where they both maintained 3.0 grade point averages on a four-point scale. After they graduated, they began taking classes in fashion design at the Art Institute of Florida. In October 1999 Serena showed off her knowledge at a fashion show in Paris. While looking at a designer top, she told a reporter, "This is a French seam."[48] A reporter noted that bit of fashion expertise in a news story that explained how the sisters had brought more fashionable styles to tennis, including the brightly colored beads they wore in their hair.

The closeness of the sisters made them naturals as women's doubles partners—a format matching two players of the same sex against another like duo—and enabled them to make more sister history. In June 1999, they won the French Open women's doubles championship by beating Martina Hingis and Anna Kournikova 6–3, 6–7, 8–6 to become just the second pair of sisters to win a Grand Slam title. The first were Grace and Ellen Roosevelt, cousins of President Franklin D. Roosevelt, who won the 1890 U.S. National Championships in women's doubles. The historic victory, however, was only a consolation for having failed to win the singles title. Serena showed her disappointment when she noted, "I'm sure anyone who says they would prefer to win the doubles title [instead of a singles title], they would have to be mentally unsound."[49]

Winning a Grand Slam singles title marks someone as a great player. And Venus and Serena were in a family race to be the first sister to win one.

Serena Triumphant

During the 1999 season, Serena began to show the promise her father had predicted when he said she would be better than Venus. Although the five-foot, nine-inch (1.75m) Serena was four inches (10cm) shorter than Venus, she was more muscular and could hit as powerfully as her older sister. In fact, they were both among the strongest, hardest-serving, most athletic women players the game had ever seen.

As Serena kept improving, she found that Venus was one of her toughest opponents, and in April they met for the title in the Lipton Championships in Key Biscayne, Florida. In the first championship match between sisters since nineteen-year-old Maud Watson had defeated her twenty-six-year-old sibling, Lilian, to win Wimbledon in 1884, Venus triumphed 6–1, 4–6, 6–4. Serena said she did not play well but added, "I definitely look forward to another final with Venus."[50] The loss dropped Serena to 0–3 lifetime against Venus in pro matches, but she would finally beat her older sister in another championship matchup. In October, Serena defeated Venus 6–1, 3–6, 6–3 in Munich, Germany, in the Grand

Slam Cup. Afterward they embraced, and Serena defended her sister by claiming, "I don't think Venus played that great today."[51]

Despite the satisfaction of finally having beaten Venus, it was an earlier title Serena won that was much more important. In September she had upstaged Venus by winning the U.S. Open to become the first of the two sisters to capture a Grand Slam title. At first it looked like the two sisters would be facing each other for

A Presidential Phone Call

Serena Williams's victory was the first in a Grand Slam by an African American in decades. Arthur Ashe won Wimbledon in 1975, but a black woman had not done so since Althea Gibson won the U.S. Open in 1958. Gibson was present at the Open, and Serena said she was glad the black pioneer in women's tennis had been on hand to see her win the same tournament; the sixty-two-year-old former star even hefted the big trophy Serena won. The victory electrified the sports world not only because Serena was African American, but because she was only seventeen. More people than usual had watched the match on television to see if Serena could make history. Among them was the president of the United States. During her postmatch news conference, President Bill Clinton phoned Serena. The conversation was reported in *Tennis* magazine:

> President Clinton: "Congratulations. We're proud of you. Tell your family I want y'all to come to the White House. You have a lot of fans there."
>
> Serena: "Really?"
>
> President Clinton: "We were thrilled. I mean, the whole White House was out there cheering for you."
>
> Serena: "Wow, I'm so excited. We're definitely going to make a trip."

Stephen Tignor, "Made in America," *Tennis*, November 1999, p. 85.

Serena Williams hoists the 1999 U.S. Open trophy. At seventeen she became the first black woman to win a Grand Slam title since Althea Gibson in 1958.

the title as they breezed through the early rounds of play. But when Venus lost a dramatic semifinal match to Martina Hingis 6–1, 4–6, 6–4, Serena wound up facing her sister's conqueror for the title.

On September 12, just two weeks before her eighteenth birthday, Serena upset Hingis 6–3, 7–6 to become the fifth-youngest champion in U.S. Open history. Serena claimed that part of her motivation against Hingis was that she wanted to beat the player who had knocked her sister out of the tournament. "Venus was so bummed," Serena said, "and that encouraged me to be even tougher out there."[52] When Serena finally downed Hingis, a rowdy crowd of twenty-two thousand fans erupted with screams of joy over her victory. So did Serena. But afterward, she told reporters she was so excited she could not remember what she had done to celebrate: "'Should I scream, should I yell or should I cry?' And I guess I ended up doing them all[.]"[53]

Serena added to her dramatic win the next day by teaming with Venus to win the women's doubles title as they defeated Chanda Rubin and Sandrine Testud 4–6, 6–1, 6–4. Although Serena said she played hard to make sure her sister also got a title, the 1999 U.S. Open was the tournament in which she finally surpassed her sister's accomplishments. On the eve of her title match, Serena had told reporters that she enjoyed being the Williams sister in the center of the spotlight for the first time. She even stated boldly that "I touch everyone. Everyone wants to see me. I don't blame them: Got to get a look at Serena."[54] The younger Williams sister was reveling in the fact that she was a little sister no more.

Chapter 4

The Serena Slam

The U.S. Open title Serena Williams won in 1999 was both a joy and a sorrow for her mother. Oracene Williams was happy her youngest daughter had succeeded in winning a Grand Slam title but dismayed that Venus was miserable because she had failed to accomplish the feat first. "It was almost like a death for Venus," Oracene said. "She thinks since she's the oldest, she should've been the first."[55] Oracene also told reporters she thought Serena's triumph could spur Venus to work harder so she could regain her top spot in the family tennis hierarchy. Serena, however, did not think her victory would adversely affect Venus. When a reporter asked Serena if Venus would be upset that she had won a Grand Slam event first, she said she did not think it mattered because she and Venus would both have many opportunities to win Grand Slam titles. Serena also noted that the Open had not been the Grand Slam title Venus coveted the most: "It's really amazing. I was always the one to say, 'I want to win the U.S. Open. I want it.' Venus always wanted Wimbledon. I guess when she wins Wimbledon, she's going to have the same feeling."[56]

Serena and her mother were both right about Venus. But what Serena failed to foresee was that Venus's quest for Grand Slam titles would lead to some heart-wrenching losses of her own to her older sister.

Venus beat Serena in the 2000 Wimbledon semifinal. The next day Venus beat Lindsey Davenport in the final.

Venus Rising

Venus's renewed dedication and determination to improve paid off in July 2000 when she won Wimbledon. But the joy Venus felt in capturing her favorite Grand Slam tournament was dimmed by the fact that to do it she had to beat Serena in a semifinal match. After the 6–2, 7–6 victory, Venus admitted, "It's really bitter[sweet]. But someone had to move on. It was either going to be me or Serena. In this instance, it was me."[57] Although Serena had led 4–2 in the second set, she kept making mistakes after that to give the match to Venus. The next day, Venus beat defending champion Lindsay Davenport 6–3, 7–6 to become only the second black woman after Althea Gibson to win the sport's most prestigious tournament. Just two days later, Venus and Serena made more history by being the first sisters to win the tournament's women's doubles championship.

In September Venus won the U. S. Open for her second Grand Slam title, giving her one more than Serena, and in 2001 she captured both those tournaments again. Her victory in the 2001 U.S. Open was historic as Venus and Serena became the first sisters to face each other in the title match. After Venus defeated Serena 6–2, 6–4, she leaned across the net on the tennis court, hugged Serena, and told her, "I love you."[58]

Losing to Venus was not as devastating for Serena as falling to another opponent because the sisters always rejoiced in each other's successes. But because Serena was a fierce competitor, the loss still bothered her. It also made Serena determined to step up her game so she could keep pace with her older sister's accomplishments. In January 2001, while playing in a tournament in Australia, she had told a reporter she wanted to become not just a better player but the best in the world: "I am determined to take my game to a new level this year. I have done well, but professionally, not as well as I would like. I see myself as doing so much better. I'm not even halfway to where I want to get. I really want to get to the top."[59]

Both sisters had always believed they were talented enough to be the top-ranked player in the world. Tennis rankings are based on points players accumulate in tournaments, especially Grand

In 2000 Venus and Serena became the first sisters to win the Wimbledon women's doubles championship.

Serena, Venus, and Tiger

Serena Williams and her sister Venus are often compared to golfer Tiger Woods. All three are African Americans who have become dominant players in sports previously ruled by whites. In addition, all three have fathers—Richard Williams and Earl Woods—who introduced them to those sports and taught them how to play at an early age. After Serena defeated Venus at Wimbledon in July 2002, a *New York Times* writer explained why the comparison is valid:

> One thing we can comprehend is the stunning juxtaposition of race and privilege. In one case, two sisters from the inner city of Compton [California] go the independent route and rise to make a shambles of the competition. In the other, a young man whose father is African-American and whose mother is Thai takes the golf world by storm. The racial part of the story is compelling because race-based exclusion is such an integral part of our nation's past and present. [In addition] Venus, Serena and Tiger represent a tremendous story about family—about parents and children. What parent wouldn't be proud of two daughters taking turns winning championships and winning with grace? Who wouldn't be proud of a son who, with grace and charm, shattered the model of a country club sport? This is an incredible time to be a fan of golf and tennis, and we had better enjoy it while we can.

William C. Rhoden, "Sports of the Times; 2 Sports Changing for Posterity," *New York Times*, July 14, 2002. www.nytimes.com/2002/07/14/sports/sports-of-the-times-2-sports-changing-for-posterity.html.

Slam events, which award the most points to winners. Venus's string of Grand Slam victories helped her reach that goal on February 25, 2002, but she held it only until March 17, when Jennifer Capriati reclaimed the top spot.

When Serena set her mind on becoming the world's best player, she knew she had to win more Grand Slam tournaments to do it.

What Serena did not know was how fast she would reach her goal and how Venus would play a major part in her rise to the number-one ranking.

The Serena Slam

In January 2002, a sprained ankle kept Serena out of the Australian Open. But in March, Serena showed how much she had improved since her 2001 U.S. Open loss to Venus by winning the Ericcson Open. And she did it in historic fashion by defeating the three top-ranked players in the world, the first time anyone had ever beaten the top three players in one tournament. She defeated third-ranked Martina Hingis in the quarterfinals, then second-ranked Venus in the semifinals, and then knocked off top-ranked Jennifer Capriati in the title match.

Most tennis tournaments are held on hard artificial surfaces, but the French Open in June is played on clay, a softer surface that makes players change the way they hit shots and maneuver the ball. Serena had always struggled on clay in the past, but she had improved so much that she won the tournament for her second Grand Slam title. Most players who win major tournaments in any sport want to win at least one more to prove that the first was not a fluke. In addition to doing that, Serena also showed again that she was now the best player in her family by beating Venus 7–5, 6–3 in the title match. Serena explained afterward why the victory was important to her: "Obviously I'm very, very happy to win another Grand Slam because I was really fighting so long. At one point, I wouldn't get past the quarters, then I got to the [2001 U.S. Open] final, maybe a semi here [or there]. But it was just discouraging. I didn't want to be a one-hit wonder. I had to get it again."[60]

That July, Wimbledon's grass courts presented another challenging surface for Serena. But Serena's new dominance, a combination of more experience playing, and her new fierce desire to be a great player, helped her win a second straight Grand Slam. And her easy 7–6, 6–3 victory in the title match once again came at the expense of her sister, who for years had dominated her. *Sports Illustrated* writer L. Jon Wertheim raved about how exciting the all-Williams final had been and wrote that "it's clear that Serena has become the best player in women's tennis."[61] That was an easy statement to make because by winning Wimbledon, Serena accumulated enough points to be ranked number one in the world. And Venus was ranked second, which made them the first sisters to hold the top two spots.

The U.S. Open in September is the last of the four annual Grand Slams. The Williams sisters showed that they deserved the top two rankings by meeting again for the title. Once again, Serena prevailed 6–4, 6–3 for her third straight title. After her victory Serena commented, "I prefer to play Venus [in a final] because that means that we have reached our maximum potential and that we'll both go home winners. For me, I'm happy to play her in the final."[62] But Venus, feeling the weight of three straight Grand Slam losses, was understandably not as happy. She said she would only play a few more tournaments in 2002 before taking time off to recover from a mentally grueling season.

In baseball, a Grand Slam is a bases-loaded home run that drives in four runs. That term was transferred to tennis and golf to refer to someone who wins the four major tournaments in each sport. So when Serena played in the 2003 Australian Open, she had a chance to make history by capturing her fourth straight major. On January 25, Serena and Venus met yet again in the title match. Although Venus had worked hard to improve and was a much tougher foe, Serena defeated her one more time in a hard-fought three sets 7–6, 3–6, 6–4. The victory made Serena only the fifth woman to hold all four Grand Slam singles titles at the same time. She told a cheering crowd after her victory, "I never get choked up, never, but I'm really emotional right now and really, really happy. I'd like to thank my mom and dad for always supporting me."[63] Then she began to cry so hard that she could not continue talking.

Because the four victories had not come in a single year, her feat was called a Serena Slam instead of a Grand Slam. The unusual designation was only fitting because both Serena and Venus were different in many ways from other players. Those differences sometimes caused the sisters problems with both fans and other players.

Serena (at right) made history at the 2003 Australian Open when she defeated Venus in the final to become only the fifth woman to hold all four Grand Slam singles titles.

Being Different

The most obvious way the Williams sisters differed from other players was the color of their skin. Although their success was universally hailed as an inspiration for blacks around the world, Serena and Venus occasionally encountered racism at tour events. The most shocking example of this occurred in March 2001 when Serena defeated Kim Clijsters 4–6, 6–4, 6–2 to win a tournament in Indian Wells, California. Before the final match, 15,000 fans booed Richard Williams and Venus when they took their seats to watch Serena play. Richard claimed later that some of them even shouted racial slurs: "When Venus and I were walking down the

stairs to our seats, people kept calling me n-----."[64] Richard raised his fist in defiance to the taunts, but his gesture only made the crowd yell louder.

During the match, the crowd lustily booed Serena while cheering loudly for Clijsters. Serena was shocked by the outbursts: "I have to believe there was some racist component to all of this. I'd never seen such terrible behavior, and I'd certainly never been on the receiving end!"[65] Serena later claimed that racism must have motivated some of the hostile reaction she got. But she battled on through the catcalls and boos to win the title for the second straight year and afterward claimed, "I won a big battle today mentally. I think a champion can come through."[66] Serena had always loved the tournament, but she and Venus vowed to never play in it again because of the way the fans had treated them.

A general view of the match between Serena and Kim Clijsters at the 2001 Tennis Masters Series in Indian Wells, California. Before the finals, the crowd of fifteen thousand people booed Richard and Venus when they arrived to cheer on Serena.

The hostile reception, however, was not entirely based on racism. Many fans were upset that Venus had backed out of a semifinals match with Serena just four minutes before it was to have started. Although Venus told officials she was suffering from heat exhaustion, some people believed Richard had forced his daughter to withdraw to ensure Serena would win the tournament for a second straight year. That theory seemed plausible to some people because of allegations that Richard had manipulated

Match Notes

Serena Williams knows that it is as important to be mentally prepared to play tennis as it is to be in top physical condition. When her father, Richard, was teaching her tennis when she was young, he often put up signs designed to inspire her or remind her of important bits of advice about how she played. As a professional, she began writing herself notes on each match she played. She used ten sticky notes to attach them to the cover of her tennis racket so she could carry them onto the court with her. They ranged from statements about God or African American history to reminders not to hit the ball so hard that she did not keep it in bounds. Many were psychological reminders designed to motivate her to play up to her potential. This match note is from her autobiography *On the Line*:

> Fear will hold U back. Champions fear nothing. Only fear God and give Him glory. Fear no man (woman). Use those legs. God gave them to U for a reason. Put your gifts to work. Take the ball on the rise. Attack the short ball—it's waiting for U!!! Show no emotion. U R black and U can endure anything. Endure. Persevere. Stand tall.

Serena Williams with Daniel Paisner, *On the Line*. Boston: Grand Central, 2009, p. 122.

his daughters' matches in the past. One accusation claimed he had ordered Serena to play poorly against Venus in the 2000 Wimbledon semifinals so Venus could win her first Grand Slam title.

Even though Richard, Serena, and Venus all denied such allegations, the charges continued to haunt them whenever the two sisters played each other or were expected to meet in a match. In fact, the two best players in the world became magnets for criticism for almost everything they did, from skipping lesser tournaments to not being more friendly with their competitors. Venus and Serena did play fewer tournaments than most players. But that was because they wanted to pursue other interests like taking classes on designing clothes and appearing on television shows. The sisters were also singled out for being less than cordial with other players even though many of their competitors also remained aloof from their peers. Serena and Venus were even attacked because they were more athletic and muscular than most players, which some people foolishly claimed was unfeminine and hurt the sport.

New York Times reporter William C. Rhoden, among others, believed part of the fan and player hostility stemmed from jealousy that Venus and Serena were winning so many tournaments and had become so famous. In September 2002 he opined, "Now they virtually own the franchise [of women's tennis]. So the best [some people] can do is criticize the Williams sisters and try to pull them back to earth."[67] And Martina Navratilova, one of the greatest tennis players ever, defended the sisters, saying, "I think they have handled [any jealousy] really well."[68] She cautioned people to reconsider such an attitude because the sisters were great athletes who were good for the game of tennis.

The sisters were even criticized for the clothes they wore when they played tennis. Until Serena and Venus, players usually wore simple white skirts and tops. But Venus and Serena began to change tennis styles by wearing daring outfits and bright colors. Serena once played while dressed entirely in pink, and at the 2002 U.S. Open she created a media frenzy with a black Lycra catsuit that looked like leather. After beating Corina Morariu in a match, Serena joked with reporters about the body-hugging outfit: "If you don't have a good figure this isn't the best outfit to wear."[69]

The volleys of criticism directed against the sisters did not bother Serena. That was because she had so much self-confidence about herself both on and off the court. After winning Wimbledon in 2002, she told reporters:

> You have to be satisfied with you and who you are. Venus and I have learned that we're satisfied and we're happy with us. We don't have any problem with anyone [who does not like us] because you have to be happy with the person inside. When you're a little bitter and a little angry, then you're going to become resentful. Instead of becoming resentful, you should go do something about it.[70]

A Fashion Star, Too

Serena Williams had done more than win a lot of tennis tournaments. Even when she failed to win, Serena was able to influence her sport with the bolder, more colorful outfits she wore while playing. Serena and Venus both competed in clothes that were more stylish than anything ever seen in tennis. As a result, they influenced the clothing styles tennis players and other athletes began wearing. Serena explains how much the sisters enjoyed doing that:

> Venus and I have a lot of fun with fashion on the tennis court. When we started playing professionally we wore our hair braided with lots and lots of white beads in them. At first, the tennis world didn't know what to make of our look. Then, just when they had gotten used to it, we switched up and sported new styles. We have adopted different hairstyles ever since. We also try different fashions on the court. In the past, tennis players usually wore a lot of white and conservative styles and colors. We bring our flair to the sport by wearing new and exciting shapes, designs and colors that we think flatter our looks. Just because everyone else wears certain brands and styles of clothes doesn't mean that you have to follow their lead.

Venus and Serena Williams with Hilary Beard, *Venus & Serena: Serving from the Hip, 10 Rules for Living, Loving and Winning*. Boston: Houghton Mifflin, 2005, p. 81.

Serena (at right) and Venus both compete in clothes that are more stylish and colorful than any seen before in tennis. They set the trend for future tennis fashions.

Serena's positive mental attitude extended to her historic clashes with her sister, especially her four straight victories in 2002 and 2003 in Grand Slam events.

Sisters First

When Serena defeated Venus in January 2003 to complete the Serena Slam, many newspaper and magazine articles ran stories about the role reversal in which Serena had become the family's dominant player. One reporter wrote that by losing, "Venus Williams had taken her now customary subservient place next to her all-conquering younger sister."[71] But even though the news media tried to portray their relationship in terms of a rivalry for family dominance, Serena never saw it that way. Serena has written that their bond as sisters was always more important to them than their tennis victories: "Venus and I are really blessed. Long before fans and reporters knew us, our parents taught us that our relationship is much more important than being successful in tennis or getting ahead in the world. Our friendship with each other and our other sisters is one of the most important and fun aspects of our lives."[72]

Chapter 5

Serena's Fall from Number One

After she completed her Serena Slam by winning the Australian Open in January 2003, the tennis world waited in breathless anticipation to see if Serena Williams could extend her Grand Slam streak in the French Open in June. If Serena won, she would be one victory away from tying the record six consecutive Grand Slam titles Martina Navratilova had captured in 1983 and 1984. Serena fought her way to the title match only to lose to Justine Henin. The tournament was difficult for Serena because many spectators booed her during her matches. The hostile reception was from Europeans who believed the United States had been wrong to invade Iraq in March. In his June 6, 2003, radio talk show, conservative political pundit Bill O'Reilly asked Mansoor Ijaz, a reporter who had attended the tournament, if "the Iraq situation and the anti-American feeling" was to blame for anger directed at Serena. Ijaz answered, "No ands, ifs or buts about that [spectators were] venting their frustration and anger about what happened over the Iraq situation at an American athlete."[73]

In July, Williams rebounded from that bitter experience to successfully defend her Wimbledon title in yet another all-sister finals. She gained revenge on Henin by beating her in the semifinals and then defeated Venus 4–6, 6–4, 6–2. Venus had suffered a pulled abdominal muscle in her semifinal victory over Kim Clijsters, and the injury forced Venus to double over in pain at times on serves. Afterward, Isha Williams said both sisters had suffered during the match, Venus physically and Serena emotionally by seeing Venus

Venus is concerned as a court doctor treats her injury in the 2003 Wimbledon singles finals. For Serena, it was emotionally difficult to defeat her sister, who played in pain.

play with such pain: "They both had it pretty . . . bad, but it might have been rougher on Serena. Playing someone you love who is in pain and still having to play your hardest because you want the [win] is a very, very difficult thing."[74]

But in just a few weeks another injury, this time to herself, and a second, deeper emotional jolt concerning another sister would plummet Serena into the worst period of her life.

Injury and Tragedy

After proving she was the best player in the world by winning five of the last six Grand Slam titles, Serena was at the peak of her fame and tennis glory. But in late July, she suffered a freak injury that threatened her number-one ranking and everything she had worked so hard to gain. Although Serena publicly stated in 2003 that she had hurt herself while practicing tennis, she revealed in her 2009 autobiography how she really injured herself:

> I was out at a club in Los Angeles, dancing and partying and having a grand old time, but the foolish part was that I was doing it in heels. [I] went into this little spin move out there on the floor and I could feel something go in my knee. I did my move and thought, "Oh, no, Serena. This can't be good."[75]

Serena's dazzling dance move caused a partial tear in the quadriceps tendon in her left knee. She had surgery on August 1 to repair the tear and doctors told her it would be two months before she could resume playing. One of the tournaments she would miss was the U.S. Open, in which she was the defending champion. Venus also sat out the Open because of an abdominal muscle pull, which meant that someone other than Venus or Serena would win the tournament for the first time since 1998.

On September 14, Serena was in Toronto with her sister Lyndrea when they received some terrible news—her sister Yetunde Price had been murdered in Los Angeles. The five Williams sisters had always been extremely close even though Yetunde, Isha, and Lyndrea had a different father. Yetunde, who was divorced and had three children, was shot to death while sitting in a sport-utility vehicle with a male friend in Compton, the Los Angeles

Serena Is Humbled

*S*ports Illustrated magazine has documented the life of Serena Williams from the time she emerged as a teenage tennis prodigy. Most articles have been glowing tributes to her talent and accomplishments. But in 2004, journalist S.L. Price wrote that Serena's loss in the title match at Wimbledon to seventeen-year-old Maria Sharapova had stripped away the aura of invincibility that Serena had built up by dominating women's tennis for several years:

> No one escapes the humbling. That's clear now. Serena Williams had been tennis's great exception for so long [that many believed if] anyone could sidestep the sport's cruelest cycle, the wheel of succession that sends up a cold-eyed teen to stalk and harry the aging champion, it would be Serena. [But] last Saturday afternoon the 22-year-old Williams felt the wheel turn [when] Sharapova, seeded 13th, beat Williams 6–1, 6–4. Over 73 minutes Sharapova stripped away Williams's armor, the hauteur [haughtiness] that has marked her in her prime, and the resulting sights and sounds were almost unimaginable: Williams slipping at the key moment of an epic rally and bouncing on her rear end; Williams, too startled to handle a laserlike Sharapova return, emitting a loud moan; Williams taking a ball on the nose after it ricocheted off

her racket; Williams, down a break point at 4–4 in the second set, slipping again, on her way to the net, and whacking a forehand wide.

S.L. Price, "Splendor on the Grass," *Sports Illustrated*, July 12, 2004, p. 47.

Serena's loss in the 2004 Wimbledon singles finals to seventeen-year-old Maria Sharapova stripped away the perceived aura of invincibility she had previously held.

suburb in which the Williams family had once lived. Serena had deeply loved the thirty-one-year-old Yetunde, who was a decade older. Serena claimed her older sister had been like a mother to her when they were growing up and a close friend and confidante in later years. To make her sister's tragic death even worse, they had spent a lot of time together recently while Serena was recovering from her knee injury and had become closer than ever.

The four Williams sisters flocked to California upon hearing the news—Serena and Lyn from Toronto, Isha from San Francisco, and Venus from the Florida home she shared with Serena. Their parents—Richard Williams and Oracene Price—also flew there from the separate homes they had owned in Florida since divorcing in 2002. A family spokesperson issued a statement that praised Yetunde as a vital part of the family: "She was our nucleus and our rock. Our grief is overwhelming and this is the saddest day of our lives."[76] Family members gathered not only to mourn their sister but to care for her three young sons—Jeffrey, Justus, and Jair. Yetunde, who had been trained as a nurse and co-owned a hair salon, had taken her mother's maiden name of Price.

Yetunde's death deeply affected Serena, who had more time than usual to brood about the tragedy because she was unable to play tennis. In her autobiography, Serena explained how lost she was after her sister's death: "The next days and weeks were a blur, and I didn't want to bother my parents or sisters to help jog my memory on this because it was such a private, painful time. By the grace of our God, Jehovah, we managed to slog through it."[77]

Her sister's death also gave Serena an excuse to extend her break from tennis. Although doctors had predicted she could be back in eight weeks, Serena would not return for eight months. Part of the reason for her long absence was that she was grieving for her sister. But Serena has admitted that she did not mind stepping away from tennis for a longer period than her recovery would take because she had so many other interests to pursue.

Serena's Other Lives

Although Venus and Serena never missed a Grand Slam event unless they were injured, they had always competed in fewer tournaments

Learning of Her Sister's Death

Serena Williams claims that one of the worst moments in her life was when she learned that her sister Yetunde Price had been shot to death in Los Angeles in September 2003. Serena was in Toronto, Canada, acting in a television show when her sister was killed. She found out what happened when she called her sister's home. In her autobiography, *On the Line*, Serena explains the overwhelming sense of loss she felt when a cousin told her that her sister was dead:

> I thought, *Gone? Tunde?* It didn't make sense. I'd just spoken to her earlier in the day. [She had] just opened her own beauty salon and was finally starting to do well with it. She was only thirty-one years old, and I know it's a cliché but she really did have her whole life ahead of her. Gone? My sister? There was just no way. It was too crazy. Too impossible. Too sad. Her [three] children needed her. Her parents needed her. Her sisters needed her. Her baby
>
>
>
> baby baby baby [as the youngest of five sisters, that is what Serena called herself] sister needed her.

Serena Williams with Daniel Paisner, *On the Line*. Boston: Grand Central, 2009, p. 158.

Family tragedy struck when Venus and Serena's older sister, thirty one-year-old Yetunde Price, was shot to death in Compton, California, while sitting in her car.

each year than most players. Some players and tennis officials criticized them for their limited schedules, claiming that the sisters were so popular that their absence was hurting the growth of their sport's fan base. That same criticism had also been leveled at golfer Tiger Woods, another African American who drew huge crowds to the relatively few tournaments he chose to play in. Venus, Serena, and Tiger were able to play fewer tournaments because they made so much more money than most players. All three were so talented that they earned a lot of money in the few tournaments they chose to play in, and they earned additional income from endorsements. In 2004 when Serena signed a five-year $40 million contract with Nike to lend her name to a new line of tennis shoes and clothes, she made so much money that the amount she could earn just by playing tennis seemed almost trivial.

Serena in 2004 also ventured into the fashion world by starting her own designer clothing line; she named the company Aneres, which was her first name spelled backwards. In an interview, Serena showed the same brash confidence she displayed in playing tennis to describe how talented she was in designing clothes:

> I'm an unbelievable designer. I don't know how I know and just do these things. I just start sketching and then I just know the colors and I always know the forecast. I know green and purple are going to be hot. I was born to be a designer. I worked hard to be a tennis player, I don't work hard to be a designer.[78]

Fashion, however, was just one of many interests Serena pursued outside of tennis. Serena once told a reporter, "I'm an actress, I'm a model and an athlete. I put athlete third on my list."[79] She and her sister Venus had both made television appearances for several years on shows like *Hollywood Squares,* and Serena began to pursue such opportunities more avidly than Venus. She had acted on *The Wayne Brady Show* and provided the voice for her appearance on the animated comedy series *The Simpsons*. Serena was so serious about acting that she once turned down a chance to act in *Wimbledon*, a film starring Kirsten Dunst. "Playing a part in a tennis movie isn't challenging for me at all," Serena haughtily told a reporter. "I would like to do something that challenges my acting skills and get people to see the skills that I do have."[80]

After her surgery, Serena admitted that she was happy that her recovery would allow her to do more than just play tennis. "I love tennis [and] I really, really miss it," she told a reporter, "but in a way it is kind of a relief to see that, wow, this actually gives me a chance to do some other stuff, some acting especially."[81] And Serena had wasted no time diving into such projects—she was in Toronto when her sister died to act in the Showtime series *Street Time*. Serena played a reformed gang member set up on drug charges by a crook, a part that was expanded after her injury because she could devote more time to the show.

Serena also engaged in other media-related activities, including being the honorary starter of the Ford 400 motor race, appearing on the MTV Awards show, and playing a kindergarten teacher on ABC's *My Wife and Kids*. She also posed for the *Sports Illustrated* swimsuit edition and provided the voice of a character in the film *SpongeBob Squarepants*. When some people accused her of being more focused on such activities than getting back to tennis, she defended herself by saying, "I like that stuff. How many 21-year-olds are making the living I'm making, getting to do the things I do? I don't look at it as 'I've blown up,' so to speak. It's just that I'm not afraid to be in the public eye. That's just me."[82]

By not playing, Serena lost her number-one ranking to Kim Clijsters in mid-2003 after having held the top spot for fifty-seven weeks. And as the months dragged on, people began to question if Serena would ever return to tennis and, if she did, whether she could still be good enough to be considered the best player in her sport.

Serena Returns to Tennis

Serena has admitted her long absence from tennis was also due to the fact that she had not emotionally recovered from Yetunde's death. "I went through the motions of grieving [for Yetunde], but I was still too numb and raw to really grieve. I cried, but the tears didn't really take me anywhere,"[83] she has written. But she eventually forced herself to ignore her sorrow and begin training hard for a comeback.

Serena falls down during her loss to Sharapova at the 2004 Wimbledon tournament. Of the loss, she said, "I just didn't . . . don't know what happened."

Serena made a memorable return in late March 2004 in the Nasdaq-100 Open in Miami. She won the tournament for the third straight year by soundly whipping Elena Dementieva 6–1, 6–1 in the title match. But even though Serena won that tournament and a second in Beijing, China, she had a dismal season because she failed to win a Grand Slam event. Serena's most humbling defeat came in July when low-ranked Maria Sharapova, who was only seventeen years old, soundly whipped her 6–1, 6–4 in the title match to deny her a third straight Wimbledon championship. Serena, who had always been articulate in postgame interviews, was so shocked by the loss that she had trouble explaining it: "I just didn't . . . I don't know what happened."[84]

Her U.S. Open experience two months later in September was perhaps more aggravating than Wimbledon because she blamed her 6–2, 4–6, 4–6 quarterfinal loss to Jennifer Capriati on sloppy officiating. In the opening game of the third set, an umpire ruled a ball she hit out of bounds even though television replays showed it was an inch inside the lines and fair. The ruling denied her a point and upset her so much she went on to lose the match. In

Eight Months Away from Tennis

Serena Williams did not play a tennis tournament from July 2003 until March 2005 because of her knee injury. Although some people suspected her extended absence was mostly due to her wanting to pursue other interests, Serena has written that she had the right to do whatever she wanted while recovering from the injury:

> I worked hard to help my knee heal and to get my body back in shape. [But I also] focused on other aspects of my career—I handled my endorsements, designed clothes, studied acting, got a part on a television show, and had fun. Because it took my knee longer to heal than people expected and I was involved in some very visible activities like fashion shows and acting, a lot of people speculated that I had lost interest in tennis. Others criticized how I was managing my career. And many people wondered out loud if I would ever regain my form and come back to dominate the game. Through all of this speculating and nay-saying, Serena stayed focused on Serena. As I told you before [in the book], you can't let gossip and the negative opinions of other people pressure you into making decisions or change how you live your life.

Venus and Serena Williams with Hilary Beard, *Venus & Serena: Serving from the Hip, 10 Rules for Living, Loving and Winning.* Boston: Houghton Mifflin, 2005, p. 115.

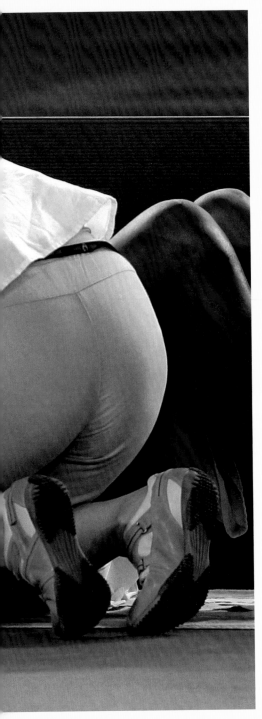

Despite a rib injury in the first set of the 2005 Australian Open, Serena went on to beat Lindsay Davenport in the finals to capture her sixth Grand Slam title.

unusually strong language Serena blasted the official, Mariana Alves: "I guess she went temporarily insane. I'm very angry and bitter right now. I just feel robbed."[85] Even though the mistake was so glaring that tournament officials apologized to Serena the next day, she had still been eliminated from the tournament.

By January 2005 when Serena played in the Australian Open, some tennis observers and players were claiming she would never again be a force in women's tennis. One of the most cutting remarks about Serena's future was made by player Jelena Dokic, who cattily claimed, "That story is over. I don't even hear comments about Serena anymore."[86] But Serena surprised everyone by regaining her old, dominating form to win the tournament. Even though she had to be treated for a rib injury during the first set, Serena vanquished Lindsay Davenport 2–6, 6–3, 6–0 to capture her sixth Grand Slam title. Afterward, Serena explained that winning another major had not been the most important thing in her life:

> We have a very, very close family. To be in some situations that we've been placed in a little over a year, it's not easy to come out and just perform at your best, especially when you realize there are so many things that are so important. I didn't think in terms of whether I would win another Grand Slam title [during my absence from tennis]. I reflected more on what was important to me in my life. I've always thought God and family were No. 1 in my life.[87]

The victory in a major, however, proved to be an aberration for Serena. She played so poorly the rest of the 2005 season that she dropped out of the top ten rankings, and 2006 was even worse: She continued to falter due to injuries and her continuing lack of ability to fully concentrate on tennis.

Still Not Ready

A major factor underlying Serena's decline was her continuing grief over the death of her sister, an emotion so strong that it sapped her will to compete. In her autobiography, this is how she describes it: "I was slipping into a depression. I don't think it was what a psychologist would have called a *clinical* depression, but it was an aching sadness, an all over weariness, a sudden disinterest in the world around me—in tennis, above all."[88]

Until Serena learned to overcome such feelings, she would be unable to regain her place as the best female tennis player in the world.

round match. Serena cried on the court because she felt so lost and unhappy. After returning to the United States, she did not play again until July. Although Serena claimed she was injured physically, the real reason she stayed away from tennis was that she was hurting emotionally. In her autobiography, Serena writes: "I was depressed. Deeply and utterly and completely depressed. I didn't talk to anyone for weeks and weeks. I think I went a month and a half without talking to my mom, which was so out of character for me because we usually spoke every day. It freaked her out, I'm sure."[91]

Her despair was a combination of her sister's death, the pressure she felt to be the world's best player, and the burden of trying to overcome a series of nagging injuries and return to tennis when she no longer cared about the sport. Eventually, she began psychological counseling in Los Angeles, where she was now living. The therapy sessions helped her look at her life and put things into perspective. So, she took a trip to Africa in November 2006 with her mom and sisters Isha and Lyn. Serena has said that seeing an island off Senegal from which Africans were shipped to the United States as slaves reminded her that, as a descendant of slaves, she could survive any hardship. "That just changed me," Serena says. "It gave me strength and courage, and it let me know that I can endure anything."[92] Serena has written that as her mood improved, she gradually began to be excited again about tennis: "All along, going back to when I was a kid, I'd never made an active or conscious choice where tennis was concerned. It was always like tennis chose me. [I] came to it by default, and it took reaching for it here, when I was down and desperate, for me fully to embrace the game. I chose tennis. At last."[93]

In January 2007, Serena took her new determination to succeed in tennis to the Australia Open. Once again, that tournament played a pivotal part in her career.

Climbing Back to Number One

Serena arrived in Australia ranked ninety-fourth in the world. She lived down to that ranking by losing to little-known Austrian Sybille Bammer in a third-round match in a minor tournament that was a warm-up for the Grand Slam event. She knew she had lost because she was out-of-shape from eating too much—she loved visiting Stand's Donuts in Los Angeles—and not exercising hard enough. So the next day she began eating less and running some steep steps in a park in Tasmania for hours to become stronger. The extra work helped her a few weeks later as she defeated Maria Sharapova 6–1, 6–2 in the Open to win her eighth Grand Slam title. Serena was so excited that she rolled on her back and kicked her legs in the air in glee. After calming down, Serena told cheering fans, "I would like to dedicate this win to my sister, who's not here. Her name is Yetunde. I just love her so much. So thanks, Tunde."[94]

The win surprised the tennis world, which had believed Serena was past her prime. But in May Serena proved that her new determination to succeed was no fluke when she won the Sony Ericsson Open in Miami by beating the world's top-ranked player, Justine Henin, in the title match. The twenty-five-year-old Williams was now boldly proclaiming that she was again the best player in the world. She told reporters, "The fact is, I love tennis. And I have an insatiable need to prove to myself that if I put my mind to it, I can do whatever I want."[95]

However, it would take her two more years of hard work and dedication to reclaim the number one ranking in tennis. Hampered again by knee and thumb injuries, Serena failed to win another tournament in 2007. But a healthy Serena won the first three tournaments of the 2008 season and in September defeated Jelena Jankovic to win the U.S. Open for her ninth Grand Slam title. The victory helped her recapture the top spot and make history—the five-year, one-month gap between her number-one rankings was a record for any player, male or female. Although Serena had done what many thought was impossible, the excitement over her amazing accomplishment did not last long: "A few minutes after I won the U.S. Open, I was like, Okay, I did that. I won. It's mine [but] the next morning, I woke up, and it was already over."[96] Serena also won a gold medal with Venus at the Beijing Olympics.

But Jankovic reclaimed the top ranking in October, and 2008 ended with Jankovic first and Serena second. That made Serena

Serena rolls on her back in joy after winning the 2007 Australian Open by defeating her nemesis Maria Sharapova. She dedicated the win to her sister Yetunde.

more determined than ever to be the best, and in 2009 she won the Australian Open and Wimbledon to claim the title of the world's best player. After winning both majors, Serena once again regained the number-one ranking she had chased for so long only to lose it in a few weeks to Dinara Safina. That happened because Serena chose not to play, and Safina won enough points to surpass her. But Serena felt she deserved some time off in a stellar year in which she had won $6,545,586 to set a new single-season earnings record. Her big year pushed her career earnings to more than $23 million, a record for a woman athlete in any sport. The Associated Press news agency named her the Female Athlete of the Year. In a story on the honor, Stacey Allaster of the Women's

Tennis Association complimented Serena by saying, "We can attribute the strength and the growth of women's tennis [in the last decade] a great deal to her. She is a superstar."[97]

In January 2010 Serena again won the Australian Open, and a few months later in April she once again regained the top ranking. And on July 3 Serena proved again she was the world's best player by winning Wimbledon for the second straight year. After easily defeating Vera Zvonareva 6–3, 6–2, Serena lifted both arms in the air in victory. She then held up all ten fingers, closed her hands, and then raised and wiggled three fingers in the air. The fingers totaled thirteen, the number of Grand Slam titles she had won in her career. Her thirteenth proved lucky as she surpassed tennis legend Billie Jean King for sixth place for the most Grand Slam singles titles by a woman player.

King was at the match and Serena jokingly told her, "Hey, Billie, I got you. This is No. 13 for me now. Its just amazing to be among such great people."[98] The win secured her place among the finest players in history. Margaret Court Smith has the most major titles (twenty-four), but Serena is only five behind U.S. great Chris Evert, who is in fifth place.

But even while Serena was regaining the number one ranking and making tennis history, she had continued to pursue the things she loved outside tennis.

A Busy Life

Many people have always wondered why Serena spends so much time doing anything other than playing tennis. This is how she answered that question in one interview:

> I have to do what I enjoy. If I want to do acting, designing or modeling, then this is who I am. It might not work for anyone else, but I need to do what I'm going to enjoy. Why stop at tennis? I'm talented at those things. I'm not going to play tennis for fifty years, but I can do other things like designing [clothes] and modeling for a long time.[99]

Serena has added jewelry items to her clothing line Aneres. "It's fabulous jewelry that I'm really proud of,"[100] claims Serena, who sometimes appears on the Home Shopping Network to sell it. With soccer star Mia Hamm and other female athletes, Serena founded Mission Skincare, a line of beauty products focused on lip, body, and sun care. Serena also showed her continuing interest in beauty and fashion by attending school in 2010 to receive her nail specialist certification. Serena told *People* magazine she was excited to take the 240-hour course because she loves doing her nails. Asked if she had any tips for her fans, she said people should "be patient! Go for long, even strokes. Use a quick-dry

Plugged-In Serena

Like many famous athletes, Serena Williams enjoys keeping in touch with her fans electronically. At her official Web site (www.serenawilliams.com), Serena blogs occasionally on various subjects from her tennis game to more personal things like her dogs, Jackie, a Jack Russell terrier, and Laurelei, a Maltese. But when Serena has something to say that she wants her fans to know about immediately, she puts out tweets so she can get immediate feedback on the subject. In an interview before the French Open in May 2010, Serena discussed tweeting:

Well, I tweet a lot. I have just really I don't know. I think it's cool. Sometimes I just tweet what's on my mind and sometimes maybe a little too much. I have a lot of fun with it. I think it's a cool way of connecting with, you know, the die hard fans. For me, I follow Green Day on Twitter, and whenever they tweet I get incredibly excited. I'm like, Oh, my God. I'm so happy and I really like to know what's going on in their lives because I'm a die hard Green Day fanatic. For those people that like me half as much as I like them, I like to keep them in the loop with my life.

Serena Williams Interview—French Open, May 24, 2010. Tennis.com. www.tennisx .com/story/2010-05-24/j.php.

Serena introduces her Aneres Collection of clothing and jewelry at The Forge restaurant in Miami, Florida, in 2004.

top coat, then stay still for 10 minutes."[101] That advice is not easy for someone as busy as Serena, who admits the classes made her busier than ever. She once spent twelve hours at the nail school, came home at 10 P.M. to work out, and then had to get up early for a 5 A.M. flight. "I really push myself to the limit," she admits.[102]

One of her favorite non-tennis activities is acting, something she would like to pursue full-time when she quits playing. Serena has made guest appearances on many television talk shows, dramas, and comedies. She and Venus even had their own reality show in 2005 titled *Venus and Serena: For Real*. One of Serena's most daring appearances was in a 2007 episode of "Fast Cars and Superstars" in which she drove a race car at 130 miles per hour (208kph) at Lowe's Motor Speedway in Charlotte, North Carolina. Serena confessed that it was the "scariest experience of my life. All of a sudden, as I was racing around the turns, I was thinking, 'This could kill me. I'm insane. What am I doing?'"[103]

Being so busy is one reason why Serena has never gotten married. Another reason stems from the advice passed down from her mother, Oracene: "When it comes to men," Oracene told a reporter, "I tell them, 'Don't get married. Don't rush yourself. Live life.' Freedom is a blessing."[104] Among the men Serena has dated are former professional football player Keyshawn Johnson and rapper Common. Neither celebrity made the grade with Serena for a long-term relationship. She and Common ended a two-year relationship in 2010, and her romance with Johnson did not last any longer. In 2003, the former all-pro receiver admitted it is difficult for sports stars to have privacy when they date: "Everybody wants to know [about you]. And I think because of who she is and who I am, and respect for her and respect for myself, we are leaving our relationship to ourselves. [Because] she's an international figure and in the United States, it's very difficult for her. But she's handled it well."[105]

Although the media can make life difficult for a celebrity, the money Serena earns allows her to help people by donating to charities and publicizing causes dear to her heart. Serena has been involved in many charities. She helped build two schools in Africa, and in 2010 she played in a charity tennis tournament in Australia to raise money for Haiti's earthquake victims. The fortune Serena has earned as a pro tennis player also allowed her in 2009 to become a part owner of the Miami Dolphins football team, which thrilled her because she loves the game so much. Venus is also a part-owner of the team.

The Williams Sisters' Legacy

In 2000, Venus and Serena went to New York to introduce dolls created in their likenesses. The dolls sold separately for $19.99 or $34.99 for the pair, and it is as a pair that they will always be remembered because their tennis careers as well as their lives as sisters always have been intricately intertwined. From 1998 to January 2010, Serena and Venus played each other in twenty-three professional matches, with Serena winning thirteen of them. Eight of those matchups were in Grand Slam finals—the first in the 2001 U.S. Open and the last in the 2010 Australian Open—and Serena has triumphed six times. In addition, the sisters have won eleven Grand Slam doubles titles together, including the 2010 Australian Open championship.

But despite their fierce tennis battles, the sisters have remained close. In June 2010, Serena was interviewed before the Wimbledon tournament began. She talked about how much she loved Venus and how she still saw her older sister as a role model. Serena also explained that the sisters' unity comes from feeling as though they were battling the nearly all-white world of tennis together: "Venus and I are really close. People always want to take us out [of a tournament] and play their super-best game against us. We are taking on these players, who, basically, find a different level when they play us. I always take it as a compliment. It's us against them."[106]

That feeling of "us against them" was born when they encountered racism as children in California because they were the only African Americans competing in tournaments. That bond strengthened after they turned professional and continued to feel the sting of prejudice from some players and fans. Their dual success in a sport previously dominated by whites has helped change tennis. Karlyn Lothery, chief diversity officer of the U.S. Tennis Association, claims, "People had a traditional thought of what tennis was

As part of their legacy, in 2000 the sisters announced the production of action-figure dolls made in their likeness.

supposed to look like. Venus and Serena changed that."[107] By winning so many important tournaments, the sisters have shown the world that blacks can succeed in tennis. And like Tiger Woods in golf, they have inspired more African American youngsters to take up a sport long neglected by blacks.

Another of their joint tennis legacies is that Serena and Venus have shown that talented players like themselves can excel even if they do not compete in as many tournaments as other players. And many believe that the fact they have limited their schedules has allowed them to keep playing longer than many of their peers,

Serena's Legacy Is Tarnished

Serena Williams's fantastic 2009 season was marred by an angry outburst she had in September at the U.S. Open. During a 6–4, 7–5 loss to Kim Clijsters, Serena exploded in anger when a line judge ruled she had made a foot fault, meaning her foot was over the baseline. The decision cost Williams a point, and she shouted obscenities at the line judge while threatening to shove a tennis ball down the judge's throat. Tennis officials fined her a record $82,500 for her rant. The profanity seemed out of character for Serena, and *Sports Illustrated* writer S.L. Price wrote that the incident was so ugly that it could forever affect the way fans and tennis historians view her:

> What I saw was her raising her racket in what looked like a menacing posture, though she may not have understood this at the time. But after having heard what she did say, she clearly was verbally threatening the lineswoman, and combined with the fact that she had a ball in one hand and was raising her racket over her head with the other, I don't blame the lineswoman for feeling a bit fearful. [She is certainly] a great player, but this is going to be a great blight on her career. No question about it.

S.L. Price, "How Does Her U.S. Open Implosion Change Serena's Legacy?" *Sports Illustrated*, September 13, 2009. http://sportsillustrated.cnn.com/2009/writers/sl_price/09/13/serena.q.a/index.html.

Serena argues with officials at the 2009 U.S. Open. She disagreed with a call and threatened to shove a ball down a judge's throat. She was fined a record $82,500.

who either burn out psychologically or fail physically by competing in too many events. Pam Shriver, who reached the 1978 U.S. Open finals as a sixteen-year-old amateur, said the sisters have shown that pacing themselves by skipping tournaments to do other things or heal minor injuries is beneficial. Sister Isha offers another theory why fewer tournaments have been good for them: "My parents encouraged the girls to be balanced all the time. You can't live a life and be totally about tennis and not have any outside interests, because [many players] did experience burnout at a very young age."[108]

In the end, however, the only legacy that concerns Serena is how she feels about herself. In a 2009 interview, she remarked, "You have to be happy with who you are. If I'm successful with who I am, whatever I look like, that's fine with me."[109] The self-assurance and confidence evident in that statement came from her loving family life and the success she has had in tennis as well as other endeavors. And those feelings are what have enabled Serena to be successful and content both in athletics and in her personal life.

Introduction: More than a Sports Superstar

1. Quoted in Billie Jean King, "Serena Williams: Serving Aces On and Off the Court," *Time*, May 10, 2010, p. 152.
2. Serena Williams with Daniel Paisner, *On The Line*. Boston: Grand Central, 2009, p. 15.
3. Quoted in Sally Jenkins, "Double Trouble," *Women's Sports & Fitness*, November/December 1998, p. 102.
4. Quoted in *Jet*, "Serena Williams Wins at U.S. Open; First Black Female Champion Since 1958," September 27, 1999, p. 51.
5. Quoted in Peter Hossli, "I Am a Thinker," Hossli.com, January 4, 2008. www.hossli.com/articles/2008/01/04/serena-williams-im-a-thinker/.

Chapter 1: Tennis: A Family Affair

6. Williams with Paisner, *On the Line,* dedication page.
7. Quoted in Sally Jenkins, "Double Trouble," p. 102.
8. Williams with Paisner, *On the Line,* p. 77.
9. Quoted in S.L. Price, "Who's Your Daddy?" *Sports Illustrated*, May 31, 1999, p. 86.
10. Williams with Paisner, *On the Line,* p. 77.
11. Venus and Serena Williams with Hilary Beard, *Venus & Serena: Serving from the Hip, 10 Rules for Living, Loving and Winning*. Boston: Houghton Mifflin, 2005, p. 3.
12. Quoted in Sonja Steptoe, "Child's Play," *Sports Illustrated*, June 10, 1991. http://sportsillustrated.cnn.com/tennis/features/williams/flashback/childs/.
13. Quoted in *Guardian* (Manchester), "Serena Williams: *Queen of the Court*: Extracts from Serena's Newly Published Autobiography," August 29, 2009. www.guardian.co.uk/sport/2009/aug/29/serena-williams-autobiography-extracts.
14. Quoted in Kim Goldstein, "Serena Williams," *Rolling Stone*, June 22, 2000, p. 114.
15. Quoted in "Mother Power! Serena and Venus on the Fabulous

Oracene, Mother of the Williams Dynasty!" *Ebony*, May2003, p. 156.

16. Quoted in Williams with Paisner, *On the Line*, p. 51.
17. Quoted in Price, "Who's Your Daddy?" p. 86.
18. Williams with Paisner, *On the Line*, p. 51.
19. Simon Hattenstone, "'There's More to Life than Hitting a Ball,'" *Guardian* (Manchester), August 29, 2009. www.guardian .co.uk/sport/2009/aug/29/serena-williams-interview.

Chapter 2: Preparing for the Pros

20. Quoted in Steptoe, "Child's Play."
21. Quoted in Williams with Paisner, *On the Line*, p. 95.
22. Quoted in Mark Peyser and Allison Samuels, "Venus and Serena Against the World," *Newsweek*, August 24, 1998. p. 44.
23. Williams with Paisner, *On the Line*, p. 103.
24. Dave Rineberg, *Venus & Serena: My Seven Years as Hitting Coach for the Williams Sisters*. Hollywood, CA: Frederick Fell, 2001, p. 7.
25. Williams with Beard, *Venus & Serena*, p. 84.
26. Williams with Paisner, *On the Line*, p. 101.
27. Quoted in Price, "Who's Your Daddy?" p. 86.
28. Quoted in Rineberg, *Venus & Serena*, p. 29.
29. Quoted in Robert McG. Thomas Jr., "Double-Barreled Debuts; Williams Sisters Join the Family Circle, *New York Times*, April 6, 1992. www.nytimes.com/1992/04/06/sports/side lines-double-barreled-debuts-williams-sisters-join-the-family-circle.html.
30. Quoted in Robin Finn, "In Tennis, Child Prodigies Whet the Agents' Appetites," *New York Times*, April 8, 1991, p. C6.
31. Quoted in Finn, "In Tennis, Child Prodigies Whet the Agents' Appetites," p. C6.
32. Quoted in Robin Finn, "Never Too Young for Tennis Millions," *New York Times*, November 10, 1993. www.nytimes.com/ 1993/11/10/sports/tennis-never-too-young-for-tennis-millions .html.
33. Quoted in Robin Finn, "Taking the Pro Plunge When Feet

Aren't Wet," *New York Times*, February 23, 1994. www.nytimes
.com/1994/02/23/sports/on-pro-tennis-taking-the-pro-plunge-
when-feet-aren-t-wet.html.

34. Quoted in Robin Finn, "Williams Tastes Victory at Prime-
Time Debut," *New York Times*, November 1, 1994. www.nytimes
.com/1994/11/01/sports/tennis-williams-tastes-victory-at-
prime-time-debut.html.

35. Quoted in Rineberg, *Venus & Serena*, p. 40.

Chapter 3: Escaping from Her Sister's Shadow

36. Williams with Paisner, *On the Line*, p. 114.

37. Quoted in Robin Finn, "Tennis: A Family Tradition at Age
14," *New York Times*, October 31, 1995. www.nytimes.com/
1995/10/31/sports/tennis-a-family-tradition-at-age-14.html.

38. Rineberg, *Venus & Serena*, p. 120.

39. Quoted in Finn, "Tennis: A Family Tradition at Age 14."

40. Quoted in Robin Finn, "Father Knew Best; Sisters Thrive Under Family Tutelage, Not Conventional Training," *New York
Times*, November 11, 1997, p. C3.

41. Quoted in Rineberg, *Venus & Serena*, p. 105.

42. Quoted in Finn, "Tennis: A Family Tradition at Age 14."

43. Quoted in George Vecsey, "Parents Were Right; Serena Could
Play, Too." *New York Times*, September 12, 1999. www.nytimes
.com/1999/09/12/sports/sports-of-the-times-parents-were-
right-serena-could-play-too.html.

44. Quoted in S.L. Price, "Martina Hingis and Patrick Rafter
Reigned at the U.S. Open, but the Play of Venus Williams Was
the Bigger Story, Much to Her Peers' Dismay," *Sports Illustrated*,
September 15, 1997. http://sportsillustrated.cnn.com/tennis/
features/williams/flashback/envy/.

45. Jenkins, "Double Trouble," p. 102.

46. Quoted in Joy Duckett Cain and Tamala Edwards, "At the Top
of Their Game," *Essence*, August 1998, p. 78.

47. Quoted in Sal A. Zanca, "Continents Apart, Williams Sisters
Make History," *New York Times*, March 1, 1999. www.nytimes
.com/1999/03/01/sports/tennis-continents-apart-williams-
sisters-make-history.html.

48. Quoted in *New York Times*, "Consolation for Williamses," June 7, 1999. www.nytimes.com/1999/06/07/sports/tennis-a-consolation-for-williamses.html.

49. Quoted in Ginia Bellafante, "Serena Williams; Game, Set, Dress Me in Leather," *New York Times*, October 17, 1999. www.nytimes.com/1999/10/17/style/shopping-with-serena-williams-game-set-dress-me-in-leather.html.

50. Quoted in L. Jon Wertheim, "We Told You So," *Sports Illustrated*, April 5, 1999, p. 68.

51. Quoted in *New York Times*, "Serena Wins Sister Act," October 4, 1999. www.nytimes.com/1999/10/04/sports/tennis-roundup-serena-wins-sister-act.html.

52. Quoted in Howard Chua-Eoan, "Her Serena Highness," *Time*, September 20, 1999, p. 58.

53. Quoted in Price, "Father Knew Best."

54. Quoted in Price, "Father Knew Best."

Chapter 4: The Serena Slam

55. Quoted in Price, "Father Knew Best."

56. Quoted in Stephen Tignor, "Made in America,"*Time*, November 1999, p. 85.

57. Quoted in Selena Roberts, "Serena Williams Was Done in by 40 Unforced Errors and the Failure to Win Big Points," *New York Times*, July 7, 2000, p. D1.

58. Quoted in Fran Metcalf, "Sister Act," *Courier Mail* (Brisbane, Australia), September 15, 2001, p. L14.

59. Quoted in Ray Kershler, "Bold Ambition; Serena Williams Plans to Take Game to Next Level," *Herald Sun* (Melbourne, Australia), January 8, 2001, p. 38.

60. Quoted in Leo Schlink, "Second Title Puts Her Mind at Rest," *Daily Telegraph* (Sydney, Australia), June 10, 2001, p. 42.

61. Quoted in L. Jon Wertheim, "Serves & FOLLIES," *Sports Illustrated*, July 15, 2002, p. 60.

62. Quoted in Selena Roberts, "Serena Williams Shows Confidence and Flair," *New York Times*, September 9, 2009. www.nytimes.com/2002/09/09/sports/tennis-serena-williams-shows-confidence-and-flair.html.

63. Quoted in Christopher Clarey, "A Slam to Call Her Own," *New York Times*, January 25, 2003, p. D1.

64. Quoted in *Jet*, "Richard Williams Laments His Tennis Star Daughters Are Subjected to Racial Slurs; Denies Rigging Their Matches," April 9, 2001, p. 51.

65. Williams with Paisner, *On the Line*, p. 79.

66. Quoted in Selena Roberts, "Serena Williams Wins as the Boos Pour Down," *New York Times*, March 18, 2001. www.nytimes.com/2001/03/18/sports/tennis-serena-williams-wins-as-the-boos-pour-down.html.

67. Quoted in William C. Rhoden, "For Sisters, Ambivalence Overshadows Performance," *New York Times*, September 7, 2002. www.nytimes.com/2002/09/07/sports/sports-of-the-times-for-sisters-ambivalence-overshadows-performance.html.

68. Quoted in George Vecsey, "Age of Enlightenment," *Tennis*, February 2002, p. 80.

69. Quoted in Thomas Whitaker, "Nice Ace, Serena!" *Sun* (London), August 28, 2002, p. 16.

70. Quoted in Selena Roberts, "Williamses Aren't Outsiders, but They're Still Different," *New York Times*, August 2, 2002. www.nytimes.com/2002/08/25/sports/tennis-williamses-aren-t-outsiders-but-they-re-still-different.html.

71. Quoted in Christopher Clarey, "Williams Sisters Complete a Role Reversal," *New York Times*, January 26, 2003. www.nytimes.com/2003/01/26/sports/tennis-williams-sisters-complete-a-role-reversal.html.

72. Williams with Beard, *Venus & Serena*, p. 3.

Chapter 5: Serena's Fall from Number One

73. Quoted in Bill O'Reilly and Mansoor Ijaz, "Personal Story," *O'Reilly Factor,* Fox News, June 6, 2003.

74. Quoted in S.L. Price, "Nerves and Volleys," *Sports Illustrated*, July 14, 2003, p. 46.

75. Williams with Paisner, *On the Line*, p. 164.

76. Quoted in Anna Cock, "Serena, Venus Suffer Greatest Loss," *Advertiser* (Adelaide, Australia), September 16, 2003, p. 3.

77. Williams with Paisner, *On the Line*, p. 161.
78. Quoted in Fox News, "Serena Williams Keen on Fashion Career," November 14, 2004. www.foxnews.com/story/0,293 3,138502,00.html.
79. Quoted in Mary Ormsby, "Death Has Sisters Pondering Future," *Toronto Star*, September 21, 2003, p. E5.
80. Quoted in Andrew Pierce, "Serena Williams," *Times* (London), June 17, 2003, p. 6.
81. Quoted in Christopher Clarey, "Williamses Test a Life Without Any Games," *New York Times*, August 28, 2003. www.nytimes .com/2003/08/28/sports/tennis-williamses-test-a-life-without-any-games.html/.
82. Quoted in Jon L. Wertheim, "The Serena Show" *Sports Illustrated*, May 26, 2004, p. 36.
83. Williams with Paisner, *On the Line*, p. 166.
84. Quoted in S.L. Price, "Splendor on the Grass," *Sports Illustrated*, July 12, 2004, p. 46.
85. Quoted in *Sports Illustrated,* "Serena Falls to Capriati amid Controversy; Roddick Continues to Roll," September 7, 2004. http://sportsillustrated.cnn.com/2004/tennis/specials/us_open/ 2004/09/07/capriati.serena.ap/index.html.
86. Quoted in Tom Fordyce, "Serena's Biggest Test," BBC Sports, January 25, 2005. http://news.bbc.co.uk/sport2/hi/tennis/ 3563759.stm.
87. Quoted in Paul Malone, "'It Means a Lot to Me to Win'; Family Guides Serena," *Sunday Mail* (Adelaide, Australia), January 30, 2005, p. 46.
88. Williams with Paisner, *On the Line*, p. 173.

Chapter 6: Serena Returns to Number One

89. Quoted in BBC.com, "Angry Williams Rejects Criticism," January 25, 2005. http://news.bbc.co.uk/sport2/hi/tennis/420 4449.stm.
90. *New York Times*, "Times Topics: Serena Williams," November 30, 2009. http://topics.nytimes.com/top/reference/timestopics/ people/w/serena_williams/index.html.
91. Williams with Paisner, *On the Line*, p. 175.

92. Quoted in Alex Tresniowski, "Serena, Serene," *People*, March 19, 2007, p. 111.

93. *Guardian*, "Serena Williams: Queen of the Court."

94. Quoted in Paul Malone, "Reduced Her Mum to Tears," *Sunday Mail* (Adelaide, Australia), January 28, 2007, p. 1.

95. Quoted in Sean Gregory, "Slam, Glam, Serena," *Time*, May 17, 2007. www.time.com/time/magazine/article/0,9171,162 2574,00.html.

96. Quoted in Chris Jones, "The Things We Forget, Part 6: Venus and Serena Williams, Their Resurgence Was Overlooked," *ESPN: The Magazine*, December 2008. http://sports .espn.go.com/espnmag/story?section=magazine&id=37 41095.

97. Quoted in Tennis.com, "Williams Wins AP's Female Athlete of the Year Award," December 22, 2009. www.tennis.com/ articles/templates/news.aspx?articleid=3024&zoneid=4.

98. Quoted in Howard Fendrich, "Adding to Greatness," *Milwaukee Journal Sentinel*, July 4, 2010, p. C3.

99. Quoted in Hossli, "I Am a Thinker."

100. Quoted in Jasymyne A. Cannick, "Serena Williams," *Ebony*, October 2008, p.73.

101. Quoted in Jackie Fields, "Training to Be a Nail Tech!" *People*, April 5, 2010, p. 140.

102. Quoted in Melody K. Hofman, "Serena's Comfort Zone." *Jet*, March 15, 2010, p. 32.

103. Quoted in Michelle Kaufman, "Serena Not to Be Taken Lightly," *Miami Herald*, March 21, 2007, p. 1.

104. Quoted in *Ebony*, "Mother Power! Serena and Venus on the Fabulous Oracene, Mother of the Williams Dynasty," May 2003, p. 156.

105. Quoted in Rick Stroud, "Bucs WR Keyshawn Johnson Discusses His Relationship with Serena Williams, the World's Top Women's Tennis Player," *St. Petersburg (FL) Times*, July 22, 2003. www.sptimes.com/2003/07/22/Bucs/A_couple _of_champions.shtml.

106. Quoted in Malcolm Folley, "It's Us Against the World," *Mail on Sunday* (London), June 20, 2010, p. 7.

107. Quoted in Bruce Schoenfeld, "The Williams Effect," *Tennis*, September 2007, p. 56.
108. Quoted in Douglas Robson, "Williamses Find Balance, Avoid Burnout," *USA Today*, June 23, 2008, p. C8.
109. Quoted in Selena Roberts, "Serena Williams Shows Confidence and Flair."

1981
On September 26, Serena Jameka Williams is born in Saginaw, Michigan.

1985
Richard Williams begins teaching his three-year-old daughter Serena how to play tennis.

1991
Richard Williams pulls Venus and Serena Williams from junior competition and in September moves his family to Florida so his daughters can enroll in the Rick Macci International Tennis Academy in Delray Beach.

1992
On April 5, Venus and Serena play against each other in an exhibition doubles match at the Family Circle Magazine Cup in Hilton Head, South Carolina. Their partners are pro tennis stars Billie Jean King and Rosie Casals.

1995
In her professional debut on October 31, fourteen-year-old Serena Williams loses to Anne Miller at the Bell Challenge in Quebec City, Canada.

1999
On March 1, Serena wins her first tournament, the Gaz de France in Paris; just hours later, Venus wins the IGA Superthrift Classic in Oklahoma City, Oklahoma; they are the first sisters to win tournaments on the same day; on September 12, seventeen-year-old Serena wins the U.S. Open for her first Grand Slam title.

2002
Serena defeats Venus in the finals of three Grand Slam events—the French Open, Wimbledon, and the U.S. Open.

2003

On January 25, in the Australian Open finals, Serena again beats Venus to become the first player since Steffi Graf in 1994 to hold all four major titles at the same time; Serena has surgery on her knee on August 1 and does not return to tennis for eight months; on September 14, Serena learns her sister, Yetunde, has been shot to death in Los Angeles.

2005

In January, Serena wins the Australian Open but plays poorly the rest of the season.

2008

In September, Serena wins the U.S. Open to reclaim the number one ranking in women's tennis.

2009

Serena wins the Australian Open and Wimbledon to solidify her claim as the world's best women's tennis player.

2010

In January, Serena successfully defends her Australian Open title to claim her twelfth Grand Slam victory; in July wins Wimbledon.

For More Information

Books

Matt Christopher, *On the Court with ... Venus and Serena Williams*. New York: Little, Brown, 2002. This book for young readers has interesting information about the Williams sisters.

Serena Williams with Daniel Paisner, *On the Line*. Boston: Grand Central, 2009. Serena's autobiography is an intimate, entertaining look at her life that is worthwhile reading for anyone interested in this tennis superstar.

Venus and Serena Williams with Hilary Beard, *Venus & Serena: Serving from the Hip, 10 Rules for Living, Loving and Winning*. Boston: Houghton Mifflin, 2005. This book includes biographical material on the Williams sisters lives as well as their comments and feelings on a wide variety of subjects.

Web Sites

Serena Williams (www.serenawilliams.com). The official Web site of the tennis superstar. It includes news reports, photographs, blogs by Serena, and links to other sites.

Sports Illustrated (http://sportsillustrated.cnn.com/tennis/features/williams/main/). This site contains information, pictures, and articles about Serena and Venus Williams that have appeared in this sports magazine.

Tennis. com (www.tennis.com/). Articles and information about Serena Williams and other players.

Women's Tennis Association (www.sonyericssonwtatour.com/page/Home/0,,12781,00.html). This site sponsored by Sony Ericsson has a biography, season and career statistics, and photographs and articles about Serena Williams.

Picture Credits

Cover: © Duncan Grove/Alamy
Al Bello/Allsport/Getty Images, 34
Allsport UK/Allsport/Getty Images, 26
AP images, 38, 43, 47, 55, 79, 85
Clive Brunskill/Allsport/Getty Images, 50, 51
Clive Brunskill/Getty Images, 72-73
Gustavo Caballero/Getty Images Entertainment/Getty Images, 82
Thomas Coex/AFP/Getty Images, 63
Phil Cole/Getty Images, 70
Richard Corkery/NY Daily News Archive/Getty Images, 42
Carl De Souza/AFP/Getty Images, 76
Julian Finney/Getty Images, 86
Robert Galbraith/Reuters/Landov, 67
Paul Harris/Online USA/Getty Images, 37
Jed Jacobsohn/Allsport/Getty Images, 56-57
Kevin Lamarque/Reuters/Landov, 65
Ken Levine/Allsport/Getty Images, 20, 30
Kevin Levine/Getty Images, 19, 35
Ken Levine/Sports Illustrated/Getty Images. 25
Brad Mangin/Sports Illustrated/Getty images, 12
Andrew Milligan/PA Photos/Landov, 8
Roberto Schmidt/AFP/Getty Images, 60
Rupert Thorpe/Online USA/Getty Images, 16

About the Author

Michael V. Uschan has written nearly eighty books, including *Life of an American Soldier in Iraq*, for which he won the 2005 Council for Wisconsin Writers Juvenile Nonfiction Award. It was the second time he had won the award. Uschan began his career as a writer and editor with United Press International, a wire service that provides stories to newspapers, radio, and television. Journalism is sometimes called "history in a hurry." Uschan considers writing history books a natural extension of the skills he developed in his many years as a journalist. He and his wife, Barbara, reside in the Milwaukee suburb of Franklin, Wisconsin.